The Ultimate Marine Recruit Training Guidebook

Nick "Gunny Pop" Popaditch

SB

Savas Beatie
California

Cataloging-in-Publication Data is available from the Library of Congress.

ISBN-13: 978-1-932714-73-9

05 04 03 02 01   5 4 3 2 1
First edition, first printing

Published by
Savas Beatie LLC
989 Governor Drive, Suite 102
El Dorado Hills, CA 95762

Mailing address:

Savas Beatie LLC
P.O. Box 4527
El Dorado Hills, CA 95762
Phone: 916-941-6896
(E-mail) customerservice@savasbeatie.com

Unless otherwise indicated, all photographs courtesy of the author.

Savas Beatie titles are available at special discounts for bulk purchases in the United States by corporations, institutions, and other organizations. For more details, please contact Special Sales, P.O. Box 4527, El Dorado Hills, CA 95762, or you may e-mail us at sales@savasbeatie.com, or visit our website at www.savasbeatie.com for additional information.

Front Cover: Private First Class Brandon Roach

Proudly published, printed, and warehoused in the United States of America.

To all who have earned the title,
United States Marine

The Marines' Hymn

From the Halls of Montezuma
To the shores of Tripoli;
We fight our country's battles
in the air, on land, and sea.
First to fight for right and freedom
And to keep our honor clean;
We are proud to claim the title
Of United States Marine.

Our flag's unfurled to every breeze
From dawn to setting sun;
We have fought in ev'ry clime and place
Where we could take a gun;
In the snow of far-off Northern lands
And in sunny tropic scenes;
You will find us always on the job
The United States Marines.

Here's health to you and to our Corps
Which we are proud to serve;
In many a strife we've fought for life
And never lost our nerve;
If the Army and the Navy
Ever look on Heaven's scenes;
They will find the streets are guarded
By United States Marines.

Contents

Contents, Continued

Preface

I would like to take this opportunity to thank you for having enough faith in me to pick up a copy of this book. More importantly, I want to express my appreciation for your decision to explore the possibility of becoming one of the nations finest, the United States Marines. Generations of men and women who have earned that title before you are now looking to see who among your generation will join the ranks of the few and the proud.

The instruction in this book will prepare you for Marine Recruit Training. Although it is written from a male perspective, it equally applies to females. Recruit Training is the same for ALL Marines. Also, be aware that the sequence of events and training may fluctuate slightly, but the process does not. Here is the BOTTOM LINE: The strategies and mental groundwork you will find within these pages will prepare you for success regardless of your gender, or where or when you attend Recruit Training.

Acknowledgments

There are many people who contributed to the completion of this book. I know I will forget to mention everyone who helped along this journey, but you know who you are, and I want you to know I am grateful.

The personnel of the Marine Corps Recruit Depot, San Diego, put the professional execution of their mission on open display. Matthew Lemieux provided expert photography. The Recruiters of the San Diego area answered my questions, just as they do daily for the community at large.

The top-shelf staff of my publisher, Savas Beatie, provided the necessary expertise to assist me in turning my Drill Instructor knowledge and experience as a Marine into the written word. Marketing Director Sarah Keeney helped lay much of the groundwork and provided editorial expertise, as did Veronica Kane, who preformed the final page proofing for me. Lindy Gervin helped with pre-publicity social media, and Helene Dodier is paving the way for opening a wide variety of sales channels. Production Manager Lee Merideth helped design the book and the many charts and tables within. All of them are quiet, patient professionals. I also want to thank Managing Director Theodore P. Savas and his staff for their tireless efforts with this trigger-puller-turned-author.

I would also like to thank the Marines who make this process work he Recruiters and the Drill Instructors. Marine Recruiters pound the pavement every day looking for a few good men and women. Persistent and professional, they display Marine character in our communities. The Drill Instructors are the best of The Corps. If you cannot o, The Corps does not allow you to teach. They demonstrate by their own example the highest standards of what being a Marine is all about.

Finally, I want to thank my own Recruiter and Drill Instructors for finding me and then changing my life.

Last but never least, I want to thank my wife April, and my sons Richard and Nicholas Jr., for their support throughout this journey of our lives together.

Nick "Gunny Pop" Popaditch
May 2012
Chula Vista, California

Introduction

Young Americans enlist in the United States Marine Corps for many reasons. However, the Hollywood and pop-culture versions usually fall into two categories: new recruits are either (1) hard-core criminals to whom a judge gives the choice of "jail or the Corps," or (2) everybody's All-American team captain/class president who was conceived to lead Marines in battle. In reality, a recruit platoon is as diverse as the nation it defends.

My own story: I wasn't a leader, of criminals or athletes. Although I had done well in school, I was doing nothing after graduation. I was 18 going on 18, headed nowhere in life, slowly. I had never even met a real-life Marine.

One day, the phone rang in my parents' home. This was before caller ID, or I probably wouldn't have answered it. I picked up and heard this:

"This is Corporal Delegal from the world's finest, the United States Marine Corps. What have you been doing since high school?"

"Nothing," I replied.

He scheduled an appointment for me to come down to his recruiting office and find out what the Marine Corps was all about. I agreed, but only because I was too scared to say no, and at meeting time I didn't show.

The phone rang. This one I can't blame on no caller ID. I knew who it was. I just didn't know how to think under duress and stress—yet. Again, I picked up.

"This is Corporal Delegal from the world's finest, the United States Marine Corps. Wait there. I'm coming over."

I was too scared to leave.

Twenty minutes passed, and then I heard loud, sharp knocking on the front door. I slimed over to receive my fate. Corporal Delegal would surely punch me in the face for standing him up. I didn't even know what a Corporal was, but certainly he had the authority to make me do push-ups. I opened the door.

He didn't yell at me or punch me. Instead, he spoke in a "You have no idea what you almost missed out on" manner. Corporal Delegal then instructed me on what being a Marine was all about. This all sounded great—except there was no way I was tough enough to make it through Marine Boot Camp.

"If you don't quit on us, we will never give up on you," he replied. All I needed was a desire to be a United States Marine and the determination to not quit or give up, no matter how tough it got.

"I can do that," I thought. I not only graduated from Marine Recruit Training, but 12 years later I returned to the Marine Corps Recruit Depot to become a Drill Instructor.

The truth is, a recruit platoon has recruits of every race, creed, and religion and from every walk of life. The one thing they all have in common is a desire to become a United States Marine!

Chapter 1

Why Join the Marine Corps Instead of Other Branches?

"Most people spend their lives trying to make a difference.
Marines don't have that problem."

—President Ronald Reagan

Why would anybody want to become a Marine?

I can answer that with a single word, one that will surprise many of you: *character*. The Marines offer what I call "The Win-Win Scenario."

In 1775, the Continental Congress established two battalions of Marines. The Corps has been winning our nation's battles since the days of our founding. From the Halls of Montezuma (a reference to the Mexican-American War) to the shores of Tripoli (a reference to our fight against Barbary pirates in the early 1800s off the coast of Africa), Marines have discovered the key to success on the battlefield. And that key is *character*.

John Glenn
NASA

Character wins in combat. In other words, the better man will always prevail. The equipment carried on your body is secondary to the values and ethos contained within the Marine. *The Marine Corps trains character.*

Whether or not you arrive at Recruit Training with any character whatsoever, you will leave with the core values and ethos of a United States Marine. In return, the Marine Corps gets a resilient decision-maker, a leader who will be victorious in every climate and place. You get the character required to do that, and you carry it with you for the rest of your life. I call that a win-win scenario.

Character isn't just useful on a battlefield. It will make you better at everything else you do in life. Take a look around your neighborhood, your community, your nation. If you scratch the surface even a little, you will find that Marines are leaders in every walk of life. United States Senators Zell Miller and John Glenn are both Marines. Senator Glenn was also an astronaut, one of the men who led the world into space. Former heavyweight boxing world champion Ken Norton also earned the title Marine, as did NFL running back Mike Anderson, who honed his skills in the Camp Pendleton League. The Ultimate Fighting Championship's Brian Stamm, Hollywood's Rob Riggle and Drew Carey, and recording artist Shaggy all served in the Corps. These are just a very few examples.

The Building Blocks of Character

Just as the Marines will build your fighting stance and teach you firing positions, your character must be built from a solid foundation. We call this foundation your "Core Values." They are Courage, Honor, and Commitment. In the civilian world, these values or attributes are referred to as intangibles—things you can't see, touch, smell, or taste. That is not true in Recruit Training and in the Corps. There, these attributes and values are quite tangible: visible, obvious, touchable, and TRAINABLE.

You will use these Core Values constantly and develop them just like the muscles that move your body. It's true, they aren't as easily built. You will be challenged in ways you never have been before. To learn these values, you will face things you are accustomed to avoiding. Here are a few examples:

"Stairway to Heaven"—one of many high obstacles
that will test your courage.

You will be put in situations where you
must lead your fellow Recruits.
United States Marine Corps photo by Cpl. Matthew S. Lemieux

FEAR

You will be confronted with a constant barrage of events and experiences that will scare you. The purpose is to make you confront your fears. Some of these experiences—such as the high obstacles on the confidence course—will make you fear for your physical safety. Other experiences may include the fear of telling others what to do during stressful situations. The point of these exercises, however, is always the same: *to force you to face your fears*. The more you do this, the less fear will affect you.

Through fear, you will develop your COURAGE.

STRESS

It is easy to say you are going to do the right thing. It is another thing entirely to actually *do it* when the time comes. We will put you in positions in which doing the right thing is the most difficult thing to do. We will test you to see whether you will take the easy way out. After teaching you the right thing to do, we will challenge your conviction to stick to it. A Marine's word is his bond, and there is no exception.

Through stress, you will develop your HONOR.

FRUSTRATION

You will feel frustrated all the time during Recruit Training. Success will be very infrequent during training, and very difficult to earn. You will <u>never</u> be praised, and rarely even encouraged; despite your best efforts, your team will often fall short of the goals set out for any exercise; and you will be punished frequently. This is very unusual for most young people, but it is all intentional and done to weed out the weak-minded. Anyone can say he or she has the desire to achieve X—but talk is cheap. We will frustrate you repeatedly—to see what you really have.

Through frustration, you will develop the COMMITMENT necessary to become a United States Marine.

The Marine Corps offers two things that no other branch of the military can offer you:

1. The challenge of Marine Recruit Training, and
2. The opportunity to become a United States Marine.

We don't promise you a rose garden. If you are looking for someone to *give* you things, you should look elsewhere. Marine Recruit Training will teach you to achieve and *earn* things on your own, not just during training but for the rest of your life.

You will choose us if you want to be one of the nation's finest. We won't give you anything.

Who Should Join?

Anyone who has the COURAGE to take the oath of enlistment and the HONOR and COMMITMENT to be true to his word

Recruiting Poster
United States Marine Corps

should join the Marines. Don't forget the win-win scenario I discussed earlier. You will arrive as a civilian; but if you have the desire to see it through, you will leave as a United States Marine, complete with the ethos and core values passed down by more than 230 years' worth of our nation's finest.

Note: During Recruit Training, never look directly at (or "eyeball") your Drill Instructors unless you are given the command "Eyeballs!" Only then will you look at them. In this book, EYEBALLS! graphics offer information you should read very closely and understand. Here's the first one:

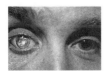 **EYEBALLS!**—The Oath of Enlistment: "I, (name), do solemnly swear (or affirm) that I will support and defend the Constitution of the United States against all enemies, foreign and domestic; that I will bear true faith and allegiance to the same and that I will obey the orders of the President of the United States and the orders of the officers appointed over me, according to regulations and the Uniform Code of Military Justice. So help me God."

What Physical Shape Should You Be in When You Join?

One of my biggest fears prior to shipping out was the physical conditioning requirement. The Recruiters tested me after my enlistment physical and discovered that I could only do one pull-up. You read that right: ONE PULL-UP. "You need to work on this," they advised me. I took their recommendation to heart and worked on it. I also began running daily. By the time of my ship date I could do three pull-ups. On my final Physical Fitness Test (PFT) at Recruit Training I could do 20 pull-ups.

So what kind of shape do you need to be in to enlist in the Marines? My example proves you can be in just about any shape, even bad shape, and still make it through. This condition, however, will not fix itself. If you are in bad shape, take some personal initiative and start doing physical training (PT) immediately. (There will be more on both initiative and PT later in this book to explain how. It is much easier to begin than you might think.)

The more you do now, the less painful it will be later, and the more results you will achieve. I guarantee that you will leave Recruit Training in good shape. It is just a matter of how much pain you want to eliminate through good preparation.

The Top Five Reasons Why You Should Join the USMC

1. "Most people spend their lives trying to make a difference. Marines don't have that problem." —President Ronald Reagan

2. You will set yourself up for success for life. Your Marine ethos and core values will go with you when you leave the Corps, making you a leader among civilians after your enlistment.

3. You will be a better person. You will develop and build your character, your body, and your mind.

4. You will become part of something much larger than yourself. "The strength of the Marine is The Corps and the strength of The Corps is the Marine."

5. You will gain the satisfaction of achieving a tough goal, proving to yourself you have the ability to be one of the nation's finest.

One of the few and the proud.
Photo by L. K. "Sgt Kat" Opasinski

The best man will always win on the battlefield. The USMC makes the best men. Marines solve problems with character and training. For example, there was a lot of friendly fire during the 1991 Persian Gulf War. (In fact, friendly fire has been a reality of warfare since the beginning of recorded history.) Once the shooting ended, other branches tried to solve these problems by tinkering with technology. The Marine Corps uses technology, of course, but it is combined with more and better target recognition training. Why is this important? Because a trained warrior is always more accurate than any technology, and he breaks down far less often.

The point of this story is a simple one: Marines pay close attention to the human element in *every* situation.

Chapter 2

Why Basic (Recruit) Training?

"Leaders are made, they are not born.
They are made by hard effort, which is the price which all of us
must pay to achieve any goal that is worthwhile."

—Vince Lombardi

You have probably noticed already that there is something different about Marines: a quality about them that civilians don't possess. How did it get there? Marines weren't born with it.

You probably have also noticed that Marines carry themselves with pride. Why are they so proud? Marine Recruit Training will transform you from a civilian with "back on the block" attitudes into a Marine in just thirteen weeks. We don't just modify you, we re-forge you. You will look different, and you will be able to think better. But it won't be easy.

*   *   *

The following information explains the reasons why you will have to go through basic training (Recruit Training) to become a Marine.

It Will Transform You From a Raw Civilian into a Basically Trained Marine

You will not just be enlisting. Instead, you will be embarking on a new career. Think of it as a new profession. This profession of arms must be approached as you would any other profession, whether you were going to be a lawyer, a firefighter, a doctor, an electrician, or an auto mechanic. As a profession, it has a set of performance skills that must be mastered, a language of its own, and a uniform to distinguish its members.

There are many skills you must learn to become a United States Marine. Some of these, such as knowledge of Marine Corps history, will be learned in a classroom similar to a college lecture hall. Others, such as first aid, will be reinforced through repetitive

Academic classes are taught in the "House of Knowledge"

practical application, or "PracAp." Other skills, such as the tactics, discipline, and teamwork necessary to accomplish a squad ambush, for example, will be taught in a classroom, reinforced through PracAp, and abstractly instructed with close order drill.

You will also learn how to speak and look like a Marine. Our naval traditions and long history have given us a language all our own. In addition to general military terms, there is specific tactical and technical terminology to learn, and you must know Marine jargon and slang in order to communicate in the Fleet Marine Force.

Recruit Training Teaches a Wide Variety of Skills

You will learn a lot more during Recruit Training than I have mentioned thus far. A few other topics include, but are not limited to:

How to physically train
How to wear and maintain a Marine uniform
Military customs and courtesies
Core Values, Ethics, and Honor
Individual character
Teamwork
Marksmanship (Marines are the best shots in the world)
How to overcome environmental challenges
Offensive and defensive military tactics
First aid
Close combat (Marine Corps martial arts)
Rappelling
Swimming (water survival)

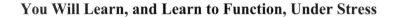
You Will Learn, and Learn to Function, Under Stress

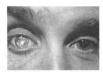

EYEBALLS! Recruit Training is all about stress. You must be able to perform every skill that you learn during Recruit Training under stressful circumstances: loud, unfamiliar, and sometimes terrifying. That is exactly how your skills will be taught, practiced, and tested: *under stress*. This will frustrate you, because you are not accustomed to learning like this. But remember: it is all about COMMITMENT—sticking with it. The reward will come in the future, when you are able to think and make clear decisions under duress—in and out of the Marine Corps.

Recruit Training will be the biggest challenge of your life. You have to learn everything I have listed, and more, under more difficult circumstances than you can probably imagine. You will be pushed to where you think your limit is—and then pushed beyond it. You will discover that your previous limits were self-imposed, and that your actual potential as a Marine is limitless.

Going through this will not be easy. Initially, fear of your Drill Instructors and forced discipline will push you. You might want to give up or quit. But your Drill Instructors will not let you. They will never give up on you—even after you have given up on yourself! During your transformation, you will reach a point when self-discipline begins to replace forced discipline. When that happens—*when self-discipline replaces forced discipline*—you will realize that pain is temporary, while the pride of succeeding is forever. Pride will replace fear as your motivation.

You will earn everything. Nothing will be easy. Most important, you have to earn the title of "United States Marine." That will not be easy—and we don't want it to be: if it were easy, everybody would do it. You will walk taller for the rest of your life because of your accomplishment.

Individual Talents and Needs versus Team Goals and Mission Accomplishment

If you have never met an actual Marine and only know the Hollywood depictions and stereotypes, you might be fearful of being turned into some sort of robot or drone. Nothing could be further from reality. Marines are thinkers—the best in the world—because we can think clearly while under extreme stress. And Marines are individuals—we have to be.

To Marines, mission comes first. Mission accomplishment is the number one priority, always. In order to do this well, we must work as a team, with every team member working toward the same goal: the mission.

If everyone on this team had the same talents and thought the same way, it might work, but not as well. With many varying talents and different minds working in the same direction, the power to accomplish is awe-inspiring. We actually count on Marines' individuality and depend on it for our success. How do we do it? We give Marines a mission, an assigned task, for everything we do. We also give them parameters through rules and regulations. Inside this box are an infinite number of possibilities to get to mission accomplishment. If you think like everyone else, you have nothing special to contribute to your team. We value your individual talents. Our team is counting on its individuals.

Many recruits have never been part of a team prior to Recruit Training, so TEAMWORK and DISCIPLINE will be taught first, and taught emphatically. Do not attempt to demonstrate your individual talents too early. Instead, prove your COMMITMENT to your team—your Recruit Training platoon. Your time will come later to exhibit your individual talents and use them to contribute to your team's success.

Good examples of individuals using their talents for a team goal can be seen everywhere. On a baseball team, the 3rd baseman has a stronger throwing arm than the 2nd baseman because he has to make a longer throw. They are positioned this way for the common goal of best defending the infield. At your high school, your social studies teacher has a better knowledge of history than your algebra teacher, who has a stronger background in mathematics. The school organized them in this manner for the common goal of best educating you. If you were injured at school, the nurse would be called, not a cafeteria server.

A Marine platoon is no different. Individuals are placed where their unique talents are best utilized for the good of the unit. Your team will be counting on you, and will draw upon your individual talents. Always going with the crowd, blending in, or doing the same as everyone else is cheating your team.

Eventually, Recruit Training will bring your individual talents out. In many cases, these will be abilities you probably did not even know you possessed. Performance skills and knowledge will be taught to you under extreme conditions and under duress. During this time-tested process, a transformation will occur. You will discover that you can physically survive adversity and think your way through frightening and complex dilemmas. Simultaneously, others around you will be discovering the same about themselves. Together you will realize that your team is capable of great things.

When you graduate, you are a Marine.

Chapter 3

You and Your Recruiter

"Never neglect details. When everyone's mind
is dulled or distracted the leader must be doubly vigilant."

—Colin Powell

A Recruiter's job is to find qualified people for the USMC. Is one of them YOU?

Once those people are identified, he wants to determine how their wants can best serve the needs of the Corps.

The basics: in order to enlist, you have to be between the ages of 17 and 28 (although it is possible to be older, under special circumstances), and medically, mentally, and morally qualified.

*   *   *

Who is Your Recruiter?

Your Recruiter will be an active-duty Marine. His job is to find qualified applicants. He is a duty expert: he knows everything about recruiting and can answer all of your questions. The Recruiter acts as the agent for both you and the Corps. Marine Recruiters are out in your communities now, "looking for a few good men."

Your Recruiter's first mission is to determine whether or not you are medically, mentally, and morally qualified to be a Marine, and he will screen you to find out.

After that, he will work on your behalf to find a place in the Corps that suits your interests and talents. Always remember, however, that the needs of the Corps come first. If this concept seems unbearable to you, you should go elsewhere. Nevertheless, the Corps has a great diversity of military occupational specialties (MOSs), and finding one that is desirable to you and that you are qualified for is generally easily accomplished.

Who Should You Believe?

Do not take as gospel your friend's advice, your teacher's advice, or Uncle Bob's advice; ASK YOUR RECRUITER.

Integrity is the most important character trait for you to embody when dealing with your Recruiter. *Integrity.* If you are not honest and direct with your Recruiter, you are wasting his time and your time. Many things that might be disqualifying can be waived or fixed, *but only if your Recruiter knows about them.*

If someone tells you, "Don't tell your Recruiter about that," do not listen; in fact, run in the opposite direction! Not only would it be unacceptable and demonstrate a lack of integrity, but it is also extremely bad advice. Withholding the truth is the same as lying, and you will be held accountable for it. If you lie to your Recruiter, you are in violation of Article 83 of the Uniform Code of Military Justice – "Fraudulent Enlistment, Appointment, or Separation." It reads as follows: "Any person who procures his own enlistment or appointment in the armed forces by knowingly false representation or deliberate concealment as to his qualifications for that enlistment or appointment and receives pay or allowances thereunder shall be punished as a court martial may direct."

Whoever gave you the bad advice will not face the consequences for this—but YOU will!

Military Entrance Processing Station

Your Recruiter will have screened you, but it is at the Military Entrance Processing Station (MEPS) that the official determination will be made whether you are medically, mentally, and morally qualified to enter the Corps. At the MEPS you will take your physical exam, your basic knowledge test, etc.

This process moves fast at times, and quite slowly at others. In the military you will frequently hear the phrase "hurry up and wait," and be prepared to "hurry up and wait" at MEPS. The key is to listen whenever someone is giving you instructions, and then

MEPS: Military Entrance Processing Station

The Oath of Enlistment

follow those instructions. When you are told to move, MOVE QUICKLY; and when you are told to wait, WAIT PATIENTLY. Always answer all questions honestly.

Your recruitment contract is put together at MEPS, and you will sign it there. If you do not understand something on your enlistment contract, *ask questions.* The Marine Corps wants you to understand this document. In fact, each portion will be explained to you, and you will not sign the contract itself until you have signed a box stating that you understand each explanation. The Marine Corps is going to hold you to this contract, so make sure you fully understand it before you sign.

After you sign your enlistment contract, you will take the oath of enlistment.

Do You Need to Be a Citizen?

This is a common question. The answer is no. If you are not a citizen, you need to be in the country legally, with valid documentation. Many join the Marine Corps seeking our core values and the challenges involved, but also the American dream.

The last two platoons I went into combat with included four Marines who were foreign nationals, from Poland, Mexico, Vietnam, and the Philippines. All were noncommissioned officers (NCOs), and three of them were on their second enlistments. We are all "Marine Corps Green." The only reason I learned they were foreign nationals was because when we returned stateside they all asked for time off to go take their citizenship tests. They are all now American citizens. Semper Fi. (This is short for "Semper Fidelis," Latin for "Always Faithful," the Marine Corps motto.)

Armed Services Vocational Aptitude Battery

The Armed Services Vocational Aptitude Battery (ASVAB) consists of a written test. It's similar to an IQ test, and is

Citizenship Ceremony

administered much like an SAT test: you will be seated at a computer, answering questions on a comprehensive test. Only the subjects will be different. It covers basic math, English, problem-solving skills, and so forth.

It is important that you do your best. Get plenty of rest the night before and eat an adequate meal before the exam. Make sure you are mentally sharp, but relax, too. Treat the test as if it were not important, but KNOW that it is. Your Recruiter will give you sample questions at his office. There are also books available to assist you with this test. I recommend *ASVAB For Dummies* by Rod Powers. Take practice tests on the internet at http://www.military.com. The ASVAB prep is found on the home page under "Resources." Both of these resources can be found at your local public library.

The ASVAB tests your aptitude in specific areas, and will be used to determine which jobs you can do in the USMC. For example, if you want to be a jet engine mechanic, you have to score high enough on the ASVAB to demonstrate the aptitude for that MOS. The higher your score, the more specialties you qualify for.

Your Enlistment Contract

Your enlistment contract will be full of complicated military jargon, legalese, etc. Here is what is important for you remember:

1. If your Recruiter promises you a specific job, you need to SEE this written in the contract—make sure it is shown to you.
2. Remember, you are agreeing to an eight-year commitment. This might be four years of active duty and four years in the inactive ready reserves. Or, you might be on active duty for all eight years, although this would be very rare. It depends on the needs of the Corps and your country.
3. When you sign the contract, you become be a "Poolee." You are agreeing to live by the terms of the contract

from then on, and you are legally accountable for your actions. You cannot get into trouble with the law, and you cannot use illegal drugs. If you do not think you can make it through this period without using drugs or getting into trouble, don't waste your time and the Corps' time by signing up at all.

4. If you change your mind after you sign up—too bad. As a Poolee, you have agreed to report back to MEPS to depart for Recruit Training on the ship date in the agreement. Your enlistment contract is a legal contract, and you have sworn an oath, so you must report for duty. This is your first opportunity to demonstrate your integrity: you made an agreement; the Marine Corps will hold you to it. Are you a man or woman of your word?

5. As a Poolee, you are a part of the Delayed Entry Program. This covers the period between your initial oath of enlistment and your ship date. Your Recruiter will be your supervisor during this period, and you must immediately inform him of any changes to your status. Always be honest with your Recruiter; do not keep any secrets from him. Do not get any new tattoos. They could be potentially disqualifying. If you get a speeding ticket—tell your Recruiter. If you get in an accident or are otherwise injured—tell your Recruiter. He can help you. Almost everything is waiverable—except lying. But if you lie to your Recruiter, we will catch you, and you will be guilty of fraudulent enlistment. Remember, you are joining an organization with a reputation for integrity: "A Marine's word is his bond." In The Corps, omission of the truth is the same as lying.

6. Your Recruiter wants you to succeed at Recruit Training. He will schedule "Poolee" functions, which are get-togethers with other Poolees in the Delayed Entry Program from your geographic area who are also preparing to ship. You will usually muster at your Recruiter's office, and then travel to the training

location. These functions can include light PT to expose you to the types you will encounter during Recruit Training. Sometimes, a Drill Instructor comes to talk about Recruit Training. At others, a Marine who has recently finished Recruit Training is made available for discussion. In addition, some of the other Poolees might be in your Recruit Training platoon, and Poolee functions are a good time to meet them. Your Recruiter understands that you have other commitments in your life at this point—work, school, family, etc.—and you might not be able to attend some of these. But these events will help you, so make every effort to attend.

7. Check in with your Recruiter at least once a week. He will never get tired of hearing from you or seeing you. Here's a tip: keep your ears open when you are around your Recruiter. Listen to how a Marine talks, and observe how he conducts himself. Never forget: everything is training, and you should always seek to improve your knowledge.

8. Be prepared for setbacks. Determining your medical, mental, and moral qualification is a detailed process that takes time. You may not accomplish it on your first try; you may not be found qualified. If this happens to you, don't be discouraged—it's not uncommon. Stay motivated, stay committed, and work with your Recruiter. Follow his instructions, and he will get you through.

Many talk about doing great things with their lives, but few do them. You are stepping up to serve your Nation, you are volunteering when you do not have to, and that is an honorable action. You have made a commitment to devote your life to this pursuit. Be proud of yourself, and use this pride to fuel you through the enlistment process.

At the completion of this phase, you will swear an oath to serve. You have started a process in motion that will improve you as a human being and commit your life to things bigger than yourself. Be proud.

Chapter 4

Value-Based Training

"It is from numberless diverse acts of courage
and belief that human history is shaped."

—Robert F. Kennedy

Everything the Marine Corps does is intended to build your character. Character is what wins in combat, so everything is designed around it. In Recruit Training, your character will be built, strengthened, and tested. By the end of Recruit Training, your character must be complete.

Your character has a body, a heart, and a spirit.

The body is HONOR.
The heart is COURAGE.
The spirit is COMMITMENT.

That is why we refer to them as Core Values. By the time you leave Recruit Training, you will embody these values, and you will be executing them with confidence.

* * *

Marines have epitomized core values throughout our history:

- During World War I at Belleau Wood in France, the Marines refused to retreat. Instead they attacked into German machine guns with such ferocity that the German defenders were routed from the woods. The Germans nicknamed them *teufel hunden*—Devil Dogs. Our French allies recognized the Marines' character in battle and awarded them the French Croix de Guerre (Cross of War).
- During the Korean War, Colonel Lewis "Chesty" Puller was in command at the Chosin Reservoir, completely surrounded by Chinese communists, outnumbered ten to one, in sub-zero weather. Colonel Puller exhibited Marine core values when he exclaimed, "They can't get away from us now!" Under his leadership, the Marines cut through the enemy—and even rescued beleaguered Army units along the way.
- During the Vietnam War, 500 Marines at the firebase at Khe Sanh were surrounded by 15,000 attacking North Vietnamese. The enemy came at the Marines relentlessly. But after 77 days, the North Vietnamese reached the conclusion that the Marines at Khe Sanh could not be defeated. They retreated, and the Marine firebase never fell.

You will learn about these Marines in history class. But learning about other Marines won't be all; you will have your own character forged in the same mold as theirs. And if you earn the distinction, you will join their ranks.

* * *

Let's examine the three Core Values and what they mean:

- **Honor:** Marines are held to the highest standards, ethically and morally. Marines never compromise what is right and just. Respect for others is essential. Marines champion the weak and oppressed and sacrifice themselves to uphold greater ideals. Marines are expected to act responsibly, in a manner befitting the title they have earned.
- **Courage:** Courage is not the absence of fear; it is the ability to face fear and overcome it. It is the mental, moral, and physical strength ingrained in every Marine. It is the resolve to follow your convictions despite danger. It steadies you in times of stress, carries you through challenge, and emboldens you to face the unknown.
- **Commitment:** Commitment is the spirit of determination and dedication found in every Marine. It is what compels Marines to place their God, their country, and The Corps ahead of themselves. It is the resolution to never accept defeat or anything less than mission accomplishment. Every aspect of life in the Corps shows commitment, from the high standard of excellence to vigilance in training.

Core Values, confidently executed, must be your bedrock. In the civilian world you are leaving, values are often called intangibles. To civilians, values are thought of as things you cannot measure, see, or touch. In the Corps, values are seen daily, close enough to touch, and you will be measured by your ability to display them.

I was commanding a tank in the first battle of Fallujah when I was severely wounded by a rocket-propelled grenade (RPG). It struck me in the head, knocked me down into the tank, and left me blind and rapidly bleeding to death. The three Marines who comprised the rest of my crew had their character put to the test. The tank's gunner, despite being wounded himself by the same

RPG, climbed up, manned my machine gun, and took command. The loader, also ignoring wounds he had sustained, continued to man his machine gun and engage the enemy. Both of these Marines did this atop a tank that was on fire from the RPG. The tank's driver, facing combat for the first time, maneuvered our burning tank out of the cramped streets of Fallujah to a Medical Evacuation point. And they had to do it quickly—before I bled out. Once there, Marines and Navy Corpsmen removed their own body armor and covered my wounded body in an effort to protect me from incoming mortar fire.

Without the Marines' Core Values embedded in their character, none of these actions would have been possible.

*   *   *

Leadership Traits

Below you will find a listing of the fourteen Leadership traits. (Chapter 5 will lay them out in more detail.) They will give you a moral compass you must use to solve moral and leadership dilemmas, both on and off the battlefield.

JUSTICE
JUDGMENT
DEPENDABILITY
INITIATIVE
DECISIVENESS
TACT
INTEGRITY
ENTHUSIASM
BEARING
UNSELFISHNESS
COURAGE
KNOWLEDGE
LOYALTY
ENDURANCE

Chapter 5 will provide you with an acronym to serve as a mnemonic (memory aid) to help you remember this list. Don't worry about it now. Just realize that you will need to memorize the traits; it is important to be able to recall them.

Other branches of the military *expose* their recruits to these traits, but the USMC *holds* their recruits to them—forever. Why? Because, taken together, these traits are what win in combat. We are here to win our nation's battles—and we do. The USMC believes that each Marine is a reflection of all Marines. Marines police each other. This is especially important because you are never off duty; you are a Marine twenty-four hours a day, seven days a week.

Here is an example of the application of the Core Values and Leadership traits. Most civilians believe that everything in the military is black and white, right and wrong. And, in fact, the *wrong* part is easy: your Core Values and numerous rules and regulations will definitely establish for you that wrong is wrong, without compromise. But the hard part is not what is wrong, but what is *right*. Frequently, especially in combat, there is more than one "right" answer. You must determine which answer is *most* right—and quickly. If you think too long, even a right decision can become wrong, because of the time it took to reach it. Core Values and the fourteen Leadership traits set a moral compass for your character—and you must have the confidence to use that compass quickly.

In the wars our country is currently facing around the world, our enemy often uses the tactic of terror in a variety of ways. For example, an enemy combatant might move close to a Marine unit dressed as a civilian, draw a concealed weapon, engage briefly, and then run away, quickly losing himself in a crowd. Your target, the fleeing enemy, will be difficult to positively identify. He will be partially covered and concealed by innocent civilians. What do you do?

There are many "right" answers, but you will have a very short time to make your decision. The enemy will be gone quickly, and if he gets away he will be a future hazard to your fellow Americans and allies. However, if the actions you choose cause harm to innocent civilians, that will likely act as a recruitment tool for the terrorists. Also, the enemy who just took a shot at you may actually be a distraction for something that hasn't happened yet. This is the moral dilemma you will face, all in the space of a few seconds.

That is why Core Values are so important, and what value-based training is all about: instilling Core Values and Leadership traits, to give the Marine a moral compass to guide him or her through moral dilemmas. This is not easy—but if it were easy, everybody would do it.

Never forget: combat is about character, and we build character. But these Core Values and Leadership traits are not just for combat. In fact, they apply to every aspect of your life, on and off the battlefield, in and out of the military. Once you earn the title Marine, you are a Marine 24/7.

Here is an example. After Recruit Training, you will receive ten days of leave to return home and visit with family and friends. During this time, while you are back among your civilian friends, they may confront you with immoral and/or unlawful behavior. Why? Because your civilian friends are not Marines, and they are not held to a higher standard.

But YOU are. In that conflict situation, will you have the honor to represent yourself and your Corps proudly? Will you have the courage to stand up, follow your moral compass, keep the commitment to your new brotherhood, and remove yourself from the bad environment? If you are a Marine, the answer will be YES.

The Fourteen Leadership Traits

"Be the change you want to see in the world."
—Mahatma Gandhi

If the Core Values we discussed are the "body, heart, and spirit" of your character, then Leadership is the "muscle" that helps it move and puts it into action. The Marine Corps will demand Leadership from you. However, up to this point in your life, it is likely that you have only rarely, if ever, been called upon to demonstrate true Leadership. You may not even know what Leadership is—yet. But don't worry, because we never send Marines into any situation unprepared. We set you up for success. The Marine Corps has been building leaders since 1775—we have it down to a science.

The Corps breaks Leadership down into 14 qualities of character. These 14 traits form the foundation of your training to be a leader.

Going in, here is one principle (from the *MC Leadership Manual*) that all Marines utilize: *know yourself and seek self-improvement.* It is easy to recognize fault in others. But to be a successful Marine, you must learn to recognize your own deficiencies and take corrective action. Your Drill Instructors will help you with this until you get the hang of it.

But you can start working on these principles and qualities *immediately.* Read, understand, and memorize these Leadership traits. You will be expected to know them and live by them. Trust me: the Marine Corps will hold you to this standard.

JUSTICE

Definition: Justice is defined as the practice of being fair and consistent. A just person gives consideration to each side of a situation and bases rewards or punishments on merit.

Suggestions for Improvement: Be honest with yourself about why you make a particular decision. Avoid favoritism. Try to be fair at all times and treat all things and people in an equal manner. It is very easy to recognize when others are unfair to you; learn to be as critical of your own actions.

JUDGMENT

Definition: Judgment is the ability to think about things clearly, calmly, and in an orderly fashion. It is what helps you make good decisions.

Suggestions for Improvement: Don't sit on the fence anymore. Weigh the facts and make a call, even on subjects or occurrences that don't interest you. Practice your ability to think through problems. Your brain is just like the muscles in your body: you have to use them to develop them. Remember, when you get to Recruit Training, you will be doing this faster, with fewer facts, and under extreme duress!

DEPENDABILITY

Definition: Dependability means that you can be relied upon to complete a job and perform your duties properly. It is the willing and voluntary support of the policies and orders of the chain of command. Dependability also means consistently putting forth your best effort in an attempt to achieve the highest standards of performance.

Suggestions for Improvement: You can increase your dependability by forming good habits: being where you're supposed to be on time; not making excuses; and carrying out every task to the best of your ability, regardless of whether you like it or agree with it.

Marines are never late. Remember, you are preparing to undertake a life-or-death profession. Practice now by arriving early to places you are supposed to be. A good rule of thumb: be fifteen minutes early. So, if you are only ten minutes early, then you are five minutes late! Arriving early to commitments allows you time to prepare for the activity to be performed. You will be ready to start on time and start at peak performance. You will be surprised at how quickly this simple practice will separate you from your peers at school and at work.

It is easy in the civilian world to carelessly give your word, and then break or bend it. End that practice right now! Make your word your bond. If people cannot trust you to accomplish simple things, how will any Marine ever be willing to trust you with his life?

INITIATIVE

Definition: Initiative is taking action even though you haven't been given orders. It means meeting new and unexpected situations with prompt action. It includes using resourcefulness to get something done without the normal material or methods being available to you.

Suggestions for Improvement: Constantly survey your surroundings. Look for things that need to be done, and DO THEM without having to be told.

DECISIVENESS

Definition: Decisiveness means being able to make good decisions without fear of getting it wrong. Good decisions incorporate good judgment and justice. Obtain available facts and weigh them against each other. Act calmly and quickly. Realize that failure to act IS a decision—a bad decision.

Suggestions for Improvement: This one is easy to state simply: MAKE MORE DECISIONS! More specifically, make more calm decisions based on facts instead of emotions.

Most importantly, realize that we have all made wrong decisions, and we will all make more wrong decisions. It's in the nature of being human. What separates the men from the boys is the ability to learn from mistakes and not fear the next decision.

 **EYEBALLS!:** INITIATIVE and DECISIVENESS are generally the two most underdeveloped traits in newly arriving recruits. So these are the two traits we work on the most to develop. During Recruit Training, you will be constantly exposed to situations that require you to utilize these traits. Even when you display good initiative and decisiveness, you may still be punished. Why? Punishment will ensure that you overcome the fear of making a mistake.

Out in the Fleet Marine Force, the only unforgivable mistake is a fear to act. A Leader's failure to act can paralyze an entire unit and risk the lives of everyone. Marines will often say, "It is better to do the wrong thing at 100 miles an hour than to do the right thing halfway."

Another expression spoken frequently in the Fleet Marine Force is: "Good initiative, bad judgment." It is a way of acknowledging that someone did right by making a decision (showing initiative), but that mistakes were made (exercising bad judgment).

Many people who are not in the military think that everything is black and white. But few things in combat will be so clearly defined, from your perspective. A Marine must have the ability to consider limited facts, remain calm, see what needs to be done, make a decision, and then carry it out. That capability makes the United States Marines the world's finest fighting force. NEVER BE AFRAID TO ACT.

TACT

Definition: Tact means dealing with people in a manner that will maintain good relations and avoid creating unnecessary problems. It means being polite, calm, and firm. Treat others with dignity and respect.

Suggestions for Improvement: Begin to develop your tact by practicing being courteous and respectful at all times. Treat others as you would like to be treated. As a United States Marine, you will always be an ambassador of the United States and a representative of the entire Marine Corps. Learn to speak and act like one.

INTEGRITY

Definition: Integrity means being honest and truthful in what you say and do. Put honesty, duty, and sound moral principles above all else.

Suggestions for Improvement: Be absolutely honest and truthful at all times. Remember that omitting the truth is the same as lying.

ENTHUSIASM

Definition: Enthusiasm is defined as a sincere interest and exuberance in the performance of your duties. If you are enthusiastic, you are optimistic, motivated, and willing to accept the challenges.

Suggestions for Improvement: Start all tasks with a positive and motivated attitude. You will be surprised at how infectious this will be to others around you. That is why this is a Leadership trait. At first you may have to force it, but soon it will become a winning habit.

Apply this habit to everything you do. Even uninteresting jobs must be done, in and out of the military. While you are in the military, whether or not you do them is not optional. But your attitude is up to you. Why do any job angry or bored?

BEARING

Definition: Bearing is the way you conduct and carry yourself. Your manner should reflect competence, confidence, dignity, control, and pride.

Suggestions for Improvement: To develop bearing, leave childish habits behind. Hold yourself to the highest standards of personal conduct. Carry yourself like a Leader, with dignity. Speak in a loud and clear tone, broadcasting confidence and competence. If you mumble something, then it was not worth saying. Speak to others with dignity (TACT).

UNSELFISHNESS

Definition: Unselfishness means that you put the needs and concerns of others ahead of your own. It means being considerate of others, and giving credit to those who deserve it. It means putting the success of your team or unit above your own personal desires and comfort—comforts and rewards are hard-earned in The Corps.

Suggestions for Improvement: Start now, learning to not seek comforts and rewards; and, even more difficult, giving them to others when you receive them. Avoid using your position for personal gain, safety, or pleasure at the expense of others.

Your Drill Instructors will teach you this trait early, often, and quite emphatically. You probably will not even recognize that the DIs are teaching you a lesson at the time; when you feel you are being personally attacked (not physically, of course), unselfishness is usually the learning objective of the lesson. Recognize it. Put your team first, and move on.

COURAGE

Definition: Courage is what allows you to remain calm and function when experiencing fear. There are two types of courage: physical and moral.

Physical courage means that you can continue to perform effectively amid physical danger. This is what most people think of when they define courage. The opportunity to demonstrate physical courage is not very common.

The other type of courage is moral courage. It means having the inner strength to stand up for what is right, and to accept blame when something is your fault. You will get more opportunities to display this type of courage.

Suggestions for Improvement: You can begin to control fear by practicing self-discipline and clear thinking. If you fear doing certain things required in your daily life, force yourself to do them until you can control your reaction. Practice moral courage by standing up for what you believe to be right. When your friends are heading down the wrong road, be the one who speaks up. You will find that the pride you feel from this display of courage is very rewarding. It will get steadily easier and easier to do, until it becomes almost second nature.

By the time you complete Recruit Training, you will have developed the discipline, identity, esprit de corps, and training of a United States Marine. All are great "fear killers."

KNOWLEDGE

Definition: Knowledge is the understanding of a science, art, or profession. It means that you have acquired information and understand how to apply it. Your knowledge should be broad: in addition to knowing your job, you should know your unit's policies. And you should constantly seek more knowledge.

Suggestions for Improvement: Increase your knowledge by developing an inquisitive mind. Listen, observe, and find out about things you don't understand. Ask lots of questions. Study the material in this book, so that when you arrive at Recruit Training you will be ahead of most of the other recruits, and able to seek new knowledge.

LOYALTY

Definition: Loyalty means that you are devoted to your religious faith, your country, The Corps, and to your seniors, peers, and subordinates. As noted earlier, the motto of our Corps is Semper Fidelis! ("Always Faithful"). You owe unwavering fidelity up and down the chain of command: to seniors, subordinates, and your peers.

Suggestions for Improvement: Train hard to become a good Marine. The generations of Marines who went before you are counting on you to uphold our traditions. You can practice now by displaying loyalty to your family.

When you begin Recruit Training, you will very quickly learn to obey orders instantaneously. At first, it will likely be fear that will motivate you to do so. In time, you will develop a respect for The Corps that will replace the fear. You will discover that other Marines will demonstrate unwavering fidelity to you. You will want to display the same fidelity to them. Both sides of this relationship will draw strength from it.

"The strength of the Marine is The Corps and the strength of The Corps is the Marine."

ENDURANCE

Definition: Endurance is mental and physical stamina, measured by your ability to withstand pain, fatigue, stress, and hardship. It is the ability to perform at high levels of mental alertness and physical performance for long periods.

Suggestions for Improvement: This one is pretty obvious. To develop endurance, do more PT. In Recruit Training, almost all PT is cardiovascular in nature. That is because no other type of exercise develops endurance quicker or more effectively, and requires no equipment to sustain and maintain.

This book will give you some basics to get started (Chapter 13). Most important, use good judgment to avoid injury—you will not be able to improve your endurance if you are hurt. But GET STARTED NOW! Your ship date will be here before you know it.

JJDIDTIEBUCKLE: In this acronym, each letter corresponds to the first letter of one of the traits. It is pronounced "J.J. DID TIE BUCKLE" (Jay Jay Did Tie Buckle), and it serves as a mnemonic (memory aid) to help you remember the 14 basic Leadership traits. By remembering the acronym, you will be better able to recall the traits. Memorize it now. Say it to yourself, and remember it.

There are two goals to Marine Corps Leadership: mission accomplishment and troop welfare:

Mission accomplishment: Anything you are told to do is your mission. It could be as simple as "Square away your footlocker" or as potentially difficult as "Capture and hold that intersection!" Mission accomplishment is what you do as a Marine. The primary goal of learning and then living these Leadership traits is so the individual can accomplish the mission.

Troop welfare: Drill Instructors will demonstrate this daily. They care about you. Their sole purpose is to train you. If they did not care, why would they be working so hard to ensure you do everything right? They know that what they are teaching you is going to help keep you—and your fellow Marines—alive on the battlefield.

Chapter 6

Things You Should Know BEFORE You Arrive

"Failing to prepare is preparing to fail."
—John Wooden

As a Marine recruit, you will be bombarded with information from day one. As noted earlier, Recruit Training is all about stress and how you handle it. You must be able to keep your mind functioning amidst a confusing barrage of distractions and physical challenges. Never forget that everything—everything—is done for a purpose. Accept that, and your training cycle will be easier.

There are some things you can and should know before you report for Recruit Training. You will put yourself well ahead of the game if you memorize naval terminology, recruit terminology, rank structure, and so on before you arrive.

Why is this important? Because it is a lot you will NOT have to worry about memorizing while the Drill Instructors are bombarding you with NEW information. If you learn it *before* you show up for Recruit Training, your mind will be free to seek new knowledge or help your fellow Recruits learn what you already know. You are demonstrating the Leadership traits *Knowledge* and *Unselfishness*—and you might just be on your way to becoming a squad leader.

Here is what you should know very well and have memorized:

The Fourteen (14) Leadership Traits: Chapter 5
Naval and Recruit Terminology: Chapter 7
General Orders: Chapter 8
Rank Structure: Chapter 9
How to Speak Like a Recruit: Chapter 10
A few select orders of the Uniform Code of Military Justice (UCMJ): Chapter 11
A basic understanding and appreciation of Marine Corps History: Chapter 12

The next several chapters will give you tips on how to organize the concepts and remember the information. Read each chapter to gain a basic understanding, but do not attempt to memorize the information the first time through. Memorization will come from steady repetition over time.

When you finish reading this, refer to the following checklist. Have it completed by your ship date. (Remember that *Dependability* is one of the 14 Leadership traits.)

Remember to be honest with yourself. The more you correct yourself, the less your Drill Instructors will have to correct you. (When they do it, it will be less pleasant and much more painful!) Put the time in NOW and arrive with a good base of knowledge.

Subject	Read Chapter	Passed Self-Test	Passed Recruiter Test
14 Leadership Traits			
Naval/Recruit Terminology			
11 General Orders			
Rank Structure			
How to Speak Like a Recruit			
UCMJ			
Marine Corps History			

Chapter 7

Recruit Terminology

"I understand a fury in your words, but not the words."
—William Shakespeare

Recruit Training is a disorienting experience. Your Drill Instructors will sound as if they are speaking a different language (and in some respects, they are). It is difficult to obey orders if you are having trouble understanding what you are being told to do or where you are being instructed to go.

The Marine lexicon (specialized vocabulary) is a combination of naval jargon, military terminology, and Marine-specific slang. When you visit a foreign country, the quicker you can speak the language, the quicker you feel comfortable; it's the same with Recruit Training.

Here are some language basics:

Directions

Port = left
Starboard = right
Fore = in front of you
Aft = behind you

You have probably noticed that these are all naval terms. This is attributable to the naval heritage of the United States Marines. Shipboard terminology is used everywhere, not just on a ship. But you will always speak as if you are on board a ship. That is how Marines speak.

THE BASE: Recruit Training Squad Bay. The Recruit who displays the most leadership is assigned as the platoon Guide. He is identified by the pictured armband and is assigned the single rack at the front of the Squad Bay.
United States Marine Corps photo by Cpl. Matthew S. Lemieux

The Base

Squad bay = the barracks (also called "the house")
Quarterdeck = the entryway to the Barracks (also called "the classroom")
Ladderwell = stairway
Deck = floor
Bulkhead = wall
Head = restroom/latrine
Scuttlebutt = drinking fountain
Hatch = door
Rack = bed
Porthole = window
Parade deck = a large area for marching and ceremonies (also called "the grinder")
Duty hut = the Drill Instructor's office
Overhead = ceiling
Colors = the national ensign (the American flag)

Uniform/Equipment Items

Cover = hat
War belt = cartridge belt worn on exterior of uniform
Knowledge = binder of Recruit Training classroom notes
Go-fasters = running shoes
PT gear = physical training uniform: shorts, t-shirt, socks, and running shoes (go-fasters); can include a sweatshirt in cold weather

A good way to learn all this is to make note cards for these terms and tape them to the corresponding items in your house. Seeing them and using the terms will help you learn, making it all second nature very quickly. By the time you report for Recruit Training, you will be speaking like an old salt.

Slang

Square away = fix or correct
Squared away = satisfactorily performing or functioning
Good to go = satisfactory
Un-sat = unacceptable in condition or performance
Back on the block = anything from your previous civilian life; generally used to describe something undesirable and undisciplined
Impact area = anywhere you have been instructed **not** to go
Portholes = glasses
Adrift = not secured or put away; scattered around
Field day = thorough cleanup
Gangway = get out of the way, clear a path
Turn to = begin a task
Secure = end a task or put away an object

This new vocabulary is all that is spoken at Recruit Training. Start working these terms into your daily speech now. Your friends might look at you a little funny, but remember moral courage: you are working on an important goal in your life. Trust me, you would rather have your friends wonder what you are doing than have your Drill Instructors not understand what you are saying—OR WORSE, HAVE YOU NOT UNDERSTAND THEM!

Self-Test

Multiple choice questions:

1. You are told to "Square away your cover." What does this mean?

   a. Make your bed
   b. Adjust your hat
   c. Turn to the right
   d. Throw out the trash

2. Where is the quarterdeck in a recruit squad bay?

    a. Immediately inside the main entrance
    b. The quarterdeck is not in the squad bay
    c. On the parade deck
    d. In the duty hut

3. Which is not included in your PT gear?

    a. Go-fasters
    b. Cover
    c. T-shirt
    d. Shorts

4. Your DI tells you to clean the Scuttlebutt. You start to clean?

    a. Porthole
    b. the Bulkhead
    c. the drinking fountain
    d. the head

5. You are facing your DI and he tells you to turn to Port. You turn:

    a. Right
    b. Aft
    c. Fore
    d. Left

The Self-Test continues on the following page.

Matching questions:

———Port	a. Stairs
———Starboard	b. Restroom
———Cover	c. Left
———Squad Bay (The House)	d. Marching area
———Head	e. Hat
———Ladderwell	f. Door
———Quarterdeck	g. Undisciplined
———Bulkhead	h. Bed
———Parade Deck (Grinder)	i. Right
———Back on the Block	j. Running shoes
———Good to go	k. Adequate
———Un-sat	l. Classroom/barracks entryway
———Squared Away	m. Fixed
———Go-fasters	n. Wall
———Rack	o. Barracks
———Hatch	p. Unacceptable

Chapter 8

The Eleven General Orders of the Sentry

"We will be brilliant on the basics."
—Vince Lombardi

The eleven General Orders of the Sentry are a building block of Marine Corps knowledge. They give guidance on exactly what to do in a wide variety of circumstances.

Have you ever noticed how confident Marines act? It comes from the reassurance that they are doing exactly what they are supposed to be doing. The eleven General Orders remove uncertainty of action.

You must know them in order, by number, and verbatim.

General Orders of the Sentry

To Take charge of this post and all government property in view.

To Walk my post in a military manner, keeping always on the alert and observing everything that takes place within sight or hearing.

To Report all violations of orders I am instructed to enforce.

To Repeat all calls from post more distant from the guardhouse than my own.

To Quit my post only when properly relieved.

To Receive, obey, and pass on to the sentry who relieves me all orders from the Commanding Officer, Officer of the Day, and Officers and Noncommissioned Officers of the Guard only.

To Talk to no one except in the line of duty.

To Give the alarm in case of fire or disorder.

To Call the Corporal of the Guard in any case not covered by instructions.

To Salute all officers and all colors and standards not cased.

To Be especially watchful at night and during the time for challenging. To challenge all persons on or near my post, and to allow no one to pass without proper authority.

Notice that every General Order starts with an action: "To [action]." The first step to memorizing your General Orders is to memorize the first two words, in order:

To take, to walk, to report, to repeat, to quit, to receive, to talk, to give, to call, to salute, to be.

After you have mastered this list of words, make eleven flashcards on 5" X 8" index cards. Put the number of the General Order and the first two words of that General Order on the front and the entire General Order on the back. Arrange them in the correct order. Practice by looking at the first two words and attempting to recite the rest without looking. After you master this, put away the flashcards and recite all eleven General Orders in sequence from memory. Finally, be able to recite a given General Order without having to state the others to get there.

Memorizing the General Orders will help you pass your Prac Test as a recruit, but *understanding* the General Orders will help you be a better recruit, and ultimately a better Marine. It is difficult to be good at something if you are unclear on exactly what you are expected to do. In the military (and as a recruit), you will often face difficult situations that have unclear solutions. Your General Orders give you *exact* guidance on what you should do.

1st General Order: Provides guidance on what you are authorized to use. If you are put in charge of something, take charge of that thing. Confidently use all assets available, assert your authority, and take initiative to use other assets nearby.

2nd General Order: Reminds you to maintain your bearing at all times, even in difficult situations. Marines are not passive bystanders, but actively alert. It also reminds you that Marines are responsible for everything they see or hear. For Marines, seeing or hearing a crime and doing nothing is the same as committing the crime.

3rd General Order: Educates you on your duty as a Marine. You are charged to report all violations, not just the ones that you think are important. Remember INTEGRITY (Chapter 5).

4th General Order: Makes clear you are never alone in the Marine Corps. It commands you to always relay communications to the next higher element in your chain of command. One of the things that makes the Marine Corps so good is that we also relay information down the chain of command. This is critical for INITIATIVE at every level. Communicate information in both directions.

5th General Order: Reminds you that Marines never quit. Anything you are told to do as a Marine or Recruit is your mission. That mission never ends until it is accomplished or until a higher authority relieves you. There are no excuses in the Marines.

6th General Order: Defines your duty as a Marine. You are required to obey all orders from your superiors. Not only must you render obedience to these orders, but you are obligated to pass them on to others who relieve you.

7th General Order: Reminds you to not be distracted from your mission.

8th General Order: Instructs you to always use your team. By the time you graduate from Recruit Training, you will be a very capable problem solver. But so will everyone else around you, so get them involved also.

9th General Order: Prompts you to notify your superiors of unusual circumstances. They have more experience than you, and will help you.

10th General Order: Instructs you to always conduct yourself as a Marine. Marines adhere to customs and courtesies and maintain discipline at all times.

11th General Order: Charges you to be at your best when times are at their worst. In the Marines, you bring your "A Game" when conditions are the most adverse.

The General Orders will apply to everything you do, not just sentry duty. Everything you are told to do by a superior is your mission as a Marine or recruit. You must receive and obey that order (6th General Order), not quit until you have accomplished it or are relieved by another (5th General Order), use all available resources to do so (1st General Order), and immediately notify your superiors if the situation changes (9th and 4th General Orders).

Memorizing and understanding the General Orders is the key to confidence and certainty of action.

Self-Test

1. Recite the eleven General Orders, from memory, in order, and verbatim.
2. Recite the even-numbered General Orders.
3. Recite the odd-numbered General Orders.

Chapter 9

Rank Structure

"I do strictly charge all personnel of lesser grade
to render obedience to appropriate orders."

—Marine Corps promotion warrant

As a recruit, everybody outranks you. You solve this rank recognition issue by referring to every Marine as "Sir" or "Ma'am." That will get you through 90 percent of Recruit Training. It will not get you through your Prac-Test, however, and will not cut it in the Fleet Marine Force. There you will be required to know Marine Corps rank structure, and because the Marines are part of the Department of the Navy, you will also be required to know Navy rank structure.

On the Prac-Test, as in the Fleet Marine force, you will be required to identify ranks by sight. In general, ranks are broken down into enlisted personnel and officers (including warrant officers). You must salute officers (remember the 10th General Order). A simple rule of thumb is that enlisted rank insignias consist of stripes (called chevrons) and rockers, while officer rank markings are generally smaller and made of shiny metal. However, if this was all you knew, you would end up saluting Navy chiefs—and looking like an untrained recruit.

To get started, review the following charts. Afterward, I'll give you tips on how to memorize them.

Enlisted Rank Structure

Marine Corps			Navy	
No Insignia	Private	E1	No Insignia	Seaman Recruit
	Private	E2		Seaman Apprentice
	Lance Corporal	E3		Seaman
	Corporal	E4		Petty Officer 3rd Class
	Sergeant	E5		Petty Officer 2nd Class
	Staff Sergeant	E6		Petty Officer 1st Class

Enlisted Rank Structure, Continued

Marine Corps				Navy
	Gunnery Sergeant	E7		Chief Petty Officer
	First Sergeant	E8		Senior Chief Petty Officer
	Master Sergeant	E8		
	Master Gunnery Sergeant	E9		Master Chief Petty Officer
	Sergeant Major	E9		

Navy Chief Petty Officer, Senior Chief Petty Officer, and Master Chief Petty Officer wear a Gold anchor with the letters USN in silver over it on the collars of certain uniforms. It looks similar to an officer's rank at a glance.

These enlisted rank markings are worn on the uniform sleeve on dress uniforms and on the collars of utility (camouflage) uniforms.

The following charts concern warrant officers and officers. Personnel of these ranks rate a salute from you. You will be instructed exactly how to do that by your Drill Instructors.

ENLISTED RANKS: Top, Marine Sergeant.
Bottom, Enlisted rank on collar.

Warrant Officer Rank Structure

Marine Corps			Navy	
	Warrant Officer 1 (Gold and Scarlet)	W-1		Warrant Officer 1 (Gold and Blue)
	Warrant Officer 2 (Gold and Scarlet)	W-2		Warrant Officer 2 (Gold and Blue)
	Warrant Officer 3 (Silver and Scarlet)	W-3		Warrant Officer 3 (Silver and Blue)
	Warrant Officer 4 (Silver and Scarlet)	W-4		Warrant Officer 4 (Silver and Blue)
	Warrant Officer 5 (Silver and Scarlet)	W-5		Warrant Officer 5 (Silver and Blue)

Officer Rank Structure

Marine Corps			Navy	
	2nd Lieutenant (Gold)	O1		Ensign (Gold)
	1st Lieutenant (Silver)	O2		Lieutenant Junior Grade (Silver)

Officer Rank Structure, Continued

Marine Corps			Navy
	Captain	O3	Lieutenant
	Major (Gold)	O4	Lieutenant Commander (Gold)
	Lieutenant Colonel (Silver)	O5	Commander (Silver)
	Colonel	O6	Captain
	Brigadier General	O7	Rear Admiral (Lower Half)
	Major General	O8	Rear Admiral (Upper Half)
	Lieutenant General	O9	Vice Admiral
	General	O10	Admiral

Review these charts to gain a general sense of the information. Once you are comfortable with that, start memorizing them. Begin by stating the rank and its description out loud. Like this:

E1 Private—no rank insignia

E2 Private First Class—one stripe up

E3 Lance Corporal—one stripe up, with crossed rifles underneath

E4 Corporal—2 stripes up, with crossed rifles underneath
and so on.

Now that you have a base of knowledge, make flashcards on 3" X 5" index cards. Draw the rank insignia on one side and its letter-number label and name on the other side. Practice these flashcards both ways. Get to the point where you can identify any given rank by sight and are able to describe a rank insignia by its rank title.

Self-Test

Mix up your flash cards. Place them not only out of rank order, but also with some forward, some backward. Test yourself with the flashcards until you get them all right, consistently.

Chapter 10

How to Speak Like a Recruit

"Courage is what it takes to stand up and speak."
—Winston Churchill

Marine Corps Recruit Training has a language all its own. You learned some of the vocabulary in Chapter 7. Now you must learn to speak like a recruit.

Military operations are very detailed and specific endeavors, so you must learn to verbalize things very specifically. In Recruit Training, every statement you make should be exact.

Pay attention to this section, and practice. When a Drill Instructor is standing in front of you and has allowed you to speak, make sure you get it right!

Rule #1: Speak LOUDLY! No one will ever tell you to quiet down. Drill Instructors like it when you sound off. It displays confidence and motivation.

Rule #2: Every Marine is a Sir or a Ma'am. Not just the Drill Instructors, but all Marines, be they enlisted or officer. You may have heard in movies this famous line: "Don't call me Sir—I work for a living." You will never hear that line on a Marine base. All Marines work hard, and you will call all Marines Sir or Ma'am. Marines understand military courtesy and respect.

This one is easy. You won't mess this one up after the first five minutes on the Recruit Depot.

Rule #3: No personal pronouns. Get rid of I, you, he, she, it, and they. These words are no longer acceptable speech in Recruit Training. Replace them with a specific description.

"I" = "This Recruit" or "Recruit (your name)"
"You" = "The Drill Instructor" or "Drill Instructor Sergeant Jones" (if you know the name)
"He/She" = "That Recruit" or "Recruit Smith" (if you know the name)
"It" = "This Recruit's rifle" or "Recruit Smith's footlocker"
"They" = "1st Squad", "the Recruits standing near the bulkhead", "this recruit's fireteam", etc.

This is not difficult to get used to doing, but you must practice because it is not your normal speech "back on the block."

Rule #4: "Yes" or "No" questions receive "Yes" or "No" answers ONLY. Do not elaborate. Have the confidence to give a simple and direct answer. Drill Instructors will ask you direct questions, not open-ended ones. Answer them accordingly. Practice this daily before arriving at Recruit Training.

Drill Instructors will never ask you an open-ended
question. Have the confidence to answer directly
when asked a direct question.
United States Marine Corps photo by Cpl. Matthew S. Lemieux

Examples:

- *You want to speak to your Drill Instructor.*

  "Recruit [your last name] requests permission to speak
  to Drill Instructor Sergeant Jones, sir."

- *You want to ask that Drill Instructor a question.*

  "This Recruit requests knowledge from the Drill
  Instructor, sir."

- *You are asked whether you have finished an assigned
  task.*

  "Yes, sir," or "No, sir." Remember, do not elaborate or
  make excuses.

Motivation is a fuel. Whenever you speak, do it LOUD, at max volume and max intensity. Nothing will seem good enough, loud enough, or fast enough for your Drill Instructors—but you will be on the right track.

Speaking like a recruit requires practice. Start by eliminating personal pronouns from your daily speech. This will make you sound funny to your family and friends (but remember the Leadership trait of COURAGE and the core value of COMMITMENT). Getting this down will set you ahead of your peers in Recruit Training. In the beginning, many recruits will be afraid to speak, and some who aren't afraid to speak will not know how to speak. But if you come in already confident in your ability to speak, you will be on your way to being a leader.

Chapter 11

The UCMJ

"Without acquaintance with the rules of propriety,
it is impossible for the character to be established."

—Confucius

Immediately after stepping off the bus at Recruit Training, you will be bombarded with information. A Drill Instructor will be shouting instructions at you and notifying you of facts that you are required to know from that moment forward.

One of these areas of knowledge will consist of selected articles from the Uniform Code of Military Justice (UCMJ). The UCMJ is military law. In addition to the laws of the United States of America and the state and city where you are stationed, you are also subject to the UCMJ.

The UCMJ differs from civil and criminal law in that it enforces honor and ethics as well as lawful conduct. It is a

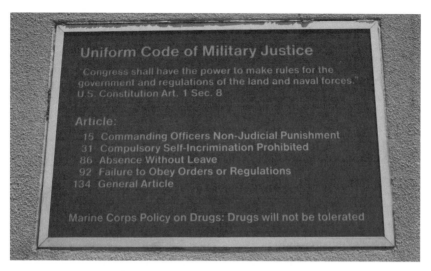

Posted UCMJ articles at Receiving Barracks.

traditional system that values morality and punishes dishonorable behavior. The UCMJ does not reward those who seek loopholes.

Do not be alarmed by this. Your life as a recruit will be very structured, and you will have few opportunities to violate the UCMJ. If you follow orders from your Drill Instructors and all other Marines, you will be fine.

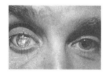

EYEBALLS! A reminder: You are subject to the UCMJ from the moment of your induction into the Marine Corps. As soon as you raise your right hand and swear the oath of enlistment, you are accountable for your actions under military law.

What follows is a brief introduction to the UCMJ, laying out some selected articles:

Article 15

Commanding Officer's Non-Judicial Punishment: Commanding officers use this article to enforce discipline for minor offenses and promote positive behavior changes without the stigma of a court-martial. This article authorizes a commanding officer to impose sanctions, such as liberty restriction, extra duties, and loss of rank, pay, and allowances upon a guilty service member. The accused can refuse this proceeding and insist on a court-martial.

Article 31

Rights of the Accused: This article states the legal rights of a Marine who has been accused of a crime. They are quite similar to the civilian equivalents. The most prominent is the protection against self-incrimination.

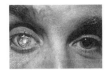 **Eyeballs**! Sea lawyer is Marine slang for a deviant who attempts to legally justify dishonorable behavior. While this sort of behavior is sometimes rewarded in civilian court, it is never tolerated under military law. The UCMJ promotes honesty, integrity, and honor. The best policy is always to be forthright and accountable for your actions. Don't be a sea lawyer. Article 31 is included in this book for your knowledge; if you find yourself actually needing to invoke your Article 31 rights during Recruit Training, you are in the wrong place.

Article 86

Unauthorized Absence (UA): This article prohibits a servicemember from leaving his appointed place of duty or failing to report to an assignment. You may be more familiar with the term AWOL; in the Marines it is called UA. Violation is punishable by a court-martial.

Article 89

Disrespect Toward a Superior Commissioned Officer: This article prohibits disrespectful behavior directed at any officer. Remember: disrespect is disrespect; it does not have to be stated out loud, it can be demonstrated silently, such as with a gesture. Violation is punishable by a court-martial.

Article 90

Assaults or willful disobedience of an order from a superior commissioned officer: This article prohibits striking, threatening to strike, or any other sort of violence against any officer, or willfully disobeying any lawful order from any officer. Violation is punishable by a court-martial. In time of war, it is punishable by death.

Article 91

Insubordination toward a noncommissioned officer: This article prohibits the striking of, any insubordinate behavior directed toward, or willful disobedience of any lawful order from a noncommissioned officer. Violation is punishable by a court-martial. The UCMJ places warrant officers and Navy petty officers in the category of noncommissioned officers.

Article 92

Failure to obey an order or regulation: This article prohibits a servicemember from disobeying any general order or regulation. This includes regulations that are known to the servicemember, even if they have not been specifically stated. For example, it is against regulations to operate a POV (any privately owned vehicle, which includes your car) on base while under the influence of alcohol. Violation is punishable by a court-martial.

Article 121

Larceny: This article prohibits a servicemember from wrongfully taking, obtaining, or withholding property from another. Violation is punishable by a court-martial.

Article 128

Assault: This article prohibits a servicemember from attempting or committing violence against another with intent to do bodily harm. Notice, one does not have to be successful to be in violation. Disobedience of this article is punishable by a court-martial. Recruit Training is not like you've seen in Hollywood movies. Keep your hands to yourself, except when training requires.

Article 134

General Article: This article is commonly referred to as the "catch-all" article. It prohibits all conduct that is unbecoming of a United States Marine: all disorders and neglects that are prejudicial to the good order and discipline of the United States Armed Forces, or of a nature to bring dishonor upon the Marine Corps. It is punishable by a court-martial.

You will notice by the numbers given here that there are over 100 articles of the UCMJ. You will not be expected to know all of them, but you will have to know the ones given here—they will be required knowledge on your Prac-Test.

You will receive academic classes on the UCMJ.

The bottom line: if you follow the orders of your Drill Instructors and conduct yourself in a manner consistent with the Core Values, you will be fine.

Chapter 12

Marine Corps History

"For the mission's sake, our country's sake, and the sake of the men who carried the Division's colors in past battles—who fought for life and never lost their nerve —carry out your mission and keep your honor clean. Demonstrate to the world there is 'No better friend, no worse enemy' than a U.S. Marine."

—General James Mattis

On November 10, 1775, the Continental Congress tasked Samuel Nicholas with raising two battalions of Marines to serve on Navy ships for ship-to-ship fighting. Nicholas went to a well-known bar in Philadelphia called Tun Tavern to find them. The bar's owner, Robert Mullens, assisted him in recruiting the first Marines. Those Marines served as ship's troops for security and boarding and as sharpshooters in ships' rigging. Early Marines wore leather collars on their uniforms to protect against sword slashes, leading to the nickname "leathernecks" which remains to this day.

Tun Tavern was the birthplace of the Marine Corps.
National Archives

During the Revolutionary War, Captain Nicholas expanded the Marines' offensive capabilities and led The Corps' first amphibious landings at New Providence in the Battle of Nassau. In actions against Barbary pirates in North Africa in the early 1800s, Marines carried our nation's flag to foreign shores. Lieutenant Presley O'Bannon led an attack in the Battle of Derna that defeated the enemy. It also began a long tradition of international appreciation of United States Marines: Lt. O'Bannon was presented with Prince Hemet's own Mameluke sword. Marine officers still wear replicas of this sword, and the battle is commemorated in *The Marines' Hymn* ("to the shores of Tripoli").

The Marines carried on their tradition of ship-to-shore fighting with a successful amphibious landing at New Orleans in the War of 1812. Marines established their precedent for leading from the front during the Mexican-American War. At the Battle of Chapultepec in 1847, 80 percent of the Marine officers and noncommissioned officers engaged were struck down. This is commemorated by the red stripe, called a blood stripe, worn down the dress blues trouser seam on officer and NCO uniforms. Marines fought with distinction during the Civil War of 1861 to 1865, and established beachheads at Guantanamo Bay, Cuba, during the Spanish-American War of 1898.

In the early 1900s, an uprising called the Boxer Rebellion occurred in China. Isolationist forces, called Boxers, attacked foreign missionaries and other Chinese citizens. Marines were called in. Dan Daly was awarded a Medal of Honor for single-handedly defending his position against relentless Boxer attacks. He inflicted over 200 casualties on the enemy. He would later be awarded a second Medal of Honor for actions in Haiti, during a series of conflicts in the first half of the 20th century in the Caribbean and Central America referred to as the Banana Wars. Successful small-unit tactics developed during the Banana Wars were the model for today's counterinsurgency operations in Afghanistan and Iraq. Gunnery Sergeant Dan Daly and Maj. Gen. Smedley Butler (Haiti and the Battle of Veracruz) are the only two Marines ever awarded the Medal of Honor twice. (General Butler was a successful author and political figure after his service. Remember the "Win-Win Scenario.")

Following the leadership of Marine pilot Lt. Alfred A. Cunningham, the Commandant established the first Marine Corps aviation company in 1915, which would evolve into the Marine air wings of today. These were distinctly different from Naval aviation: Marine pilots specialized in close air support, a tactic of attacking ground targets from the air to support advancing Marine ground units.

During World War I, the Marines arrived at Belleau Wood in France. The Germans had taken the woods and the retreating French forces advised the Marines to retreat. Captain Lloyd Williams replied, "Retreat, Hell, we just got here!" The Marines advanced into the woods into the teeth of the German defense. At the critical moment of the assault, GySgt. Dan Daly (the same one) rallied the Marines and led the attack, shouting, "Come on you sons of bitches. Do you want to live forever?" The Germans were routed from Belleau Wood. The French renamed Belleau Wood "The Woods of the Marine Brigade" and awarded the Marines the

Mitchell Paige was awarded the
Medal of Honor on Guadalcanal.
public domain

French Croix de Guerre (the cross of war, the highest French award) as thanks for saving Paris. The Germans, on their retreat, called the Marines *Teuffelhunden*, German for "devil dogs." The nickname remains to this day.

In 1918, Opha Mae Johnson broke new ground as the first female Marine. Her leadership paved the way for female Marines who served in war zones by the 1940s and the hard-charging female leathernecks of today.

On December 7, 1941, Japanese forces attacked Pearl Harbor. The United States subsequently declared war and entered into World War II. In the early days of the war, the United States suffered losses on Wake Island, Guam, and the Philippines despite valiant defenses. The Japanese succeeded in taking most of the Pacific. But the tide decisively turned with an American victory at the Battle of Midway. The arduous task of retaking the Pacific began.

The Marines started the "island-hopping" campaign. This offensive strategy consisted of taking a sequence of Pacific islands by amphibious assault. These islands were then used as airfields and ports to support the next amphibious assault on the next island. The Marines went from island to island across the Pacific to reach Japan.

Guadalcanal was the first Allied amphibious landing after American entry into World War II. After successfully taking the beach, Marines were cut off from support because naval forces were forced to withdraw. The Marines ashore fought the Japanese in the dense jungles of Guadalcanal in some of the most bitter fighting of the war. Sergeant Mitchell Paige fought off waves of bonzai charges alone with machine gun fire and led a bayonet charge counterattack that broke the enemy. He was awarded the Medal of Honor. So was Sgt. John Basilone, who pieced together machine guns and quickly organized Marines to repel numerous Japanese charges on their position. After months of fighting, the Marines secured Guadalcanal and had their first island base.

At Betio in the Tarawa Atoll, Japanese defenders were dug in and surrounded by a coral reef that blocked assault craft from landing. The Japanese commander boasted that "a million men assaulting for a hundred years could not take Tarawa." In some of the bloodiest fighting in the Pacific, Marines took Tarawa in 76 hours. It was true that the reef blocked assault boats—but not the Landing Vehicle, Tracked. This Marine amphibious tractor (amtrac) could climb over the reef on its way to the beach. Following Tarawa, the amtrac became the primary transport from ship to shore during amphibious assaults.

The closer to mainland Japan the Marines got, the deadlier the battles became. The Japanese had spent 20 years preparing the defenses on Iwo Jima. The island's 1,500 caves rendered naval bombardment ineffective. The Marines suffered 26,000 casualties during this amphibious landing, the largest to date. Gunnery Sergeant Basilone (from Guadalcanal) was killed taking the beach. He was shouting, "Come on, you bastards, we've got to get these guns off the beach" when he was killed by enemy mortar fire. When the Marines took control of Iwo Jima, they raised a flag on Mount Suribachi. That image has come to symbolize The Corps, the tough breed. Admiral Chester Nimitz said of Marines during the island-hopping campaign that "Uncommon valor was a common virtue."

With an airfield secured on Iwo Jima, the Marines next and final amphibious landing in World War II was on the Japanese island of Okinawa. Resistance was fierce. The Japanese fought to the death. It took the Marines three months to secure the island. Now mainland Japan was surrounded and blockaded. In 1945, terms of surrender were offered and refused, but then accepted following the detonation of two atomic bombs. World War II was over. The Marine Corps had made its legendary amphibious reputation in the Pacific during the island-hopping campaign.

During World War II, the Marine Corps established Montford Point. African-Americans were trained there and brought into the Corps ranks. The Marines integration of black Marines put them decades ahead of the nation they defended.

Just a few years later, The Corps was at war again. In 1950, communist North Korea attacked its neighbor, democratic South Korea. The 1st Marine Division was called into action to defend freedom. The rapid embarkation of the division reaffirmed The Corps' reputation as a "force in readiness." The Marines arrived in time to prevent the conquest of South Korea and beat the North Koreans back at the Pusan Perimeter.

John Basilone was a boxing champ in the Philippines and is sometimes called "Manila John." He was awarded the Medal of Honor on Guadalcanal and killed on the beach at Iwo Jima.

public domain

In a bold maneuver, Marines conducted an amphibious landing behind enemy lines at Inchon. If successful, this would cut the North Korean force off. It was daring because Inchon's coastline was protected from tidal variations by an eight-foot seawall. Once ashore, Marines used ladders to scale the seawall and fought their way into the city. Fighting was fierce and often hand-to-hand, but the landing succeeded—Inchon was liberated. The Marines continued to push the North Koreans back and retook South Korea's capital, Seoul, in bitter house-to-house fighting.

The 1st Marine Division continued to push north into North Korea toward the border with China. However, eight Chinese divisions reinforced the North Koreans and counterattacked near a man-made reservoir, called the Chosin Reservoir, in harsh winter weather. Army units on one flank fell, United Nations forces on the other flank collapsed, and the Marines were surrounded and outnumbered. Colonel Lewis "Chesty" Puller, a veteran of Guadalcanal and the Banana Wars, was in command. He rallied the Marines, exclaiming, "They can't get away from us now." Chesty Puller figured the Marines could shoot any direction and hit the enemy, so he ordered an attack. The Marines rallied and fought and broke out, rescuing Army units along the way. The Marines of this battle are referred to as the "Chosin few," and Chesty Puller is recognized as the Corps' most decorated Marine, a Marine icon.

In 1965, Marines landed at Da Nang to protect an airbase there that supported air operations against communist North Vietnam's aggression toward its neighbor, South Vietnam. The Vietnam War escalated. At Khe Sanh, 500 Marines defended a strategic firebase that cut off the Ho Chi Minh Trail, a vital supply route for the North Vietnamese Army (NVA) and the southern communist Viet Cong. The NVA sent 15,000 troops to knock the Marines off the hilltop firebase. After a 77-day siege, the NVA retreated back into the jungle in defeat. The Marines at Khe Sanh never fell.

During the Vietnam War, GySgt. Carlos Hathcock proved again that Marines are the best marksmen in the world. Serving as a sniper, he had 93 confirmed kills, with one at over 2,000 yards. He was so successful at his employment of a skill that Marines had handed down since sharpshooting from ships' rigging that he was tasked with establishing a formal school to instruct it.

True to the Marine tradition of commitment to mission accomplishment, Capt. John Ripley prevented 20,000 NVA from advancing on the South Vietnamese capital of Saigon. He

Chesty Puller, the Marine Corps most decorated Marine.
public domain

emplaced over 500 pounds of explosives on the Dong Ha Bridge and blew it up.

The largest engagement of the Vietnam War was the Tet Offensive, so named because it occurred during the Vietnamese New Year holiday of Tet. The North Vietnamese launched a massive, theater-wide attack into South Vietnam, largely directed at civilian population centers. Eighty thousand NVA troops surged south. The most notable battle occurred at Hue City. As the Marines had at Inchon and Seoul, they proved that house-to-house fighting in urban terrain was yet another specialty. The Tet Offensive ended with an NVA retreat, but not before the infliction of massive civilian casualties.

During the 1980s, Marines were called into action again. In 1983, Marines landed on the Caribbean island of Grenada in defense of American civilians there. Just as in the Pacific in World War II, Marines proved again that not only were amphibious operations still significant, but that Marines were the best in the world at it. The island was secured in days. Marines were utilized as an international peacekeeping force in Beirut, Lebanon. There they faced terrorist assaults and a foreshadowing of a new enemy employing new tactics. In Panama in 1989, just as on Tarawa during WWII, Marines employed a new vehicle, the Light Armored Vehicle (LAV), that proved to be the right tool for the job. The LAV's combination of firepower, mobility, and light armor provided the Marines the capability to outmaneuver the enemy and decisively engage.

On August 2, 1990, Iraq invaded its neighbor Kuwait. Iraq's quick conquest of Kuwait threatened Saudi Arabia and the stability of the entire region. As part of a United Nations coalition, the United States deployed troops, including under a previously untested program, the Maritime Prepositioned Force. Marines again proved they are a "force in readiness," arriving first on the deck with significant combat power. A counteroffensive followed to liberate Kuwait. The attack into Kuwait was led by the 1st and 2nd Marine Divisions. Within 100 hours, the Iraqis were defeated and routed from Kuwait.

Following the attacks on September 11, 2001, the United States engaged in two major campaigns. Operation Enduring Freedom was fought in Afghanistan, a landlocked country. Proving again that Marines fight "in ev'ry clime and place," they embarked on aircraft from ships over 400 miles away to establish forward operating bases in Afghanistan. The other campaign, Operation Iraqi Freedom, was fought in Iraq. It featured such heroes as Cpl.

Jason Dunham, who was awarded the Medal of Honor for selflessly sacrificing his life to save the Marines near him from a fusing-out grenade. Both these campaigns are still ongoing at this book's publication.

Marine Corps history is being written every day. When you earn the title "United States Marine," this becomes your history. It becomes your photo album. Just like in your family album, some of the pictures are of YOU. You are a part of it. Perhaps now you see why CHARACTER is taken so seriously in Recruit Training.

NOTES:
- November 10, 1775, is the Marine Corps birthdate
- Captain Samuel Nicholas was the first Commandant of the Marine Corps
- Robert Mullens was the first Marine Recruiter
- The Mameluke sword was presented to Lieutenant O'Bannon during the Barbary Pirate Wars
- Gunnery Sergeant Dan Daly and Maj. Gen. Smedley Butler are the only two Marines awarded the Medal of Honor twice
- The founder of Marine Aviation was A.A. Cunningham
- The first female Marine was Opha Mae Johnson
- The turning point of World War II was the Battle of Midway
- The strategy used in the Pacific during WWII was the "island-hopping campaign"
- The first offensive battle and amphibious landing by the Allies after American entry into World War II was at Guadalcanal
- Tarawa was the first battle in which Marines used the amphibious tractor
- Marines raised a flag on Mount Suribachi during the Battle of Iwo Jima
- The last offensive battle of WWII was at Okinawa
- Marines conducted an amphibious landing at Inchon during the Korean War despite an eight-foot seawall
- Marines fought house-to-house at Hue City during the Vietnam War

- Outnumbered Marines successfully defended Khe Sanh against a 77-day siege
- LAVs were used for the first time in Panama
- Maritime Prepositioned Forces were utilized to rapidly deploy to Saudi Arabia during the Gulf War

Marines raising the American flag on top of Mt. Suribachi, Iwo Jima, the iconic photograph of World War II.
public domain

Chapter 13

Physical Training

"If the body be feeble, the mind will not be strong."
—Thomas Jefferson

    I have spent most of this book instructing you how to prepare your mind and attitude for training. That is the most critical portion. However, if you do not establish a foundation of physical training (PT), you will arrive with a deficit you will come to regret.

    As I have told you already, you will leave Recruit Training in good shape, regardless of how you arrive. What I have not told you is that it will be physically challenging, no matter how good your condition when you arrive. The relentless pace of the training, the long hours, and the total fitness aspect will challenge your endurance, cardiovascular stamina, and durability. You must prepare your body to sustain strain and not break down.

This is hard work, but not complicated—it only requires commitment. Here are some ways to start:

Standing

Starting is simple: begin by standing more often. Things you normally do seated, begin to do them standing. For instance, read this book standing up. As with everything in this chapter, do not go from zero to 100 miles an hour overnight. Practice slow, steady progression. Stand more each day; spend more time on your feet in general. By the time you ship, standing for eight to ten hours should be normal.

This will strengthen your feet, lower body, and back. Failure to prepare yourself in this way puts you at risk for stress fractures in your legs, foot problems, and back issues.

Walking

Start putting some miles on those feet. Again, do not go from zero to 100 miles an hour right away. Start walking more miles, but add in moderation, in small increments if necessary. Take the stairs instead of the elevator; park farther away from places you go. If you have boots, wear them when you walk. Once you are comfortable walking almost everywhere, begin to open up your stride and pick up your pace. Eventually, walk everywhere you go.

You will be surprised at how fast you can get somewhere by walking.

Running

Running is the thing that's most critical to build in moderation. Build up in a slow, steady progression to your ship date. Do not run more frequently than every other day—your body must have time to recover and build. You are building more than your run time: you are strengthening your joints and bones to withstand Recruit Training; you are building your cardiovascular endurance. This increases your ability to work for longer stretches while remaining more mentally alert during that time.

Build slowly and consistently until you are running three miles without stopping. Once you can do that distance, time yourself and work on reducing your time. However, prioritize the mileage more than the time. The more miles you put on your feet prior to your ship date, the better off you will be.

Push-ups

Push-ups are a good way to build your upper-body strength. Start out by doing two sets per day, one in the morning and one in the evening, whatever number you can manage. Rest one day per week.

PUSH-UP: Start position.

PUSH-UP: Top, Keep your back straight throughout the exercise.
Bottom, Recruit Training Physical Training.

Concentrate on form. Be sure to keep your back perfectly straight throughout the entire movement. Remember, you are building more than your muscles; using perfect form strengthens your joints and bone structure, too.

Add another set each week until you are doing five sets per day, spread out throughout your day. You should be at a minimum of 20 push-ups per set and five sets per day by the time you ship.

Crunches

Crunches are best performed with a partner holding your feet, but if circumstances prevent that, put your feet under an immovable object. Start on your back with your knees bent at approximately 90 degrees and your feet flat on the deck. Place your arms across your abdomen, with each hand grasping the opposite elbow. Your arms should look similar to when you stand with your arms crossed, but not as tightly. Place something cushioned under your butt; a folded sweatshirt will do.

Without raising your butt off the ground, use your stomach muscles to lift your upper body off the ground until your forearms touch your thighs. Smoothly lower your upper body to the ground. That is one repetition.

Do crunches in conjunction with push-ups, except do twice as many crunches per set as push-ups.

CRUNCHES: Start position.

CRUNCHES: Top, Raise to up position, then return to start position.
Bottom, Prepare now. You will do lots of crunches in
Recruit Training.
United States Marine Corps photos by Cpl. Matthew S. Lemieux

Pull-ups

Pull-ups are the only preparation exercise that requires any equipment whatsoever. The good news is that a pull-up bar can be

PULL-UPS: Start position.

found just about anywhere—anything that is parallel to the deck and can support your body weight will do.

PULL-UPS: Do not stop until your chin is over the bar.

Start out doing two sets per day max. Add another set per day each week. You can do them with palms facing toward or away from you. As you improve, do sets of each type.

PULL-UPS: Can be done with palms facing away from you.

PULL-UPS: As you improve, do sets of each type.

Nothing will build your upper body strength better than pull-ups. The only way to improve your ability to do pull-ups is to do MORE pull-ups.

As you can see, none of this requires a gym membership or equipment. If you have the money, spend it on a good pair of running shoes and a good pair of walking boots. You will be able to take the running shoes to Recruit Training.

This PT program is time-tested and works well. It is also a minimum. If you play sports or do other physical things in your life, great, but do these things in addition. These exercises will prep your skeleton and joints for the rigorous training you are about to embark on. If you are committed and strictly adhere to this schedule, your body will be prepared to avoid injury, build total body fitness, and survive training in good shape.

Chapter 14

Shipping Out

"Retreat, Hell, we just got here!"
—Captain Lloyd Williams

Mindset

Let's assume you have done all the preparations suggested in this book. If so, you have prepared your mind and body for training.

As your ship date approaches, tie up loose ends. You have known your ship date for a long time, so there is no excuse for not giving proper notice at your job. The same Core Values and Leadership traits that will make you a good Marine also make you a good citizen and employee. Remember BEARING: do not use your departure as an opportunity to tell someone off, or anything like that—for that is the action of a coward. You are starting a life of honor.

You have been visiting your Recruiter, weekly at a minimum. You have ensured you have no unpaid debts, such as speeding tickets. Your family and others important in your life know you are leaving, and you have their addresses so you can write letters to them. (You need their mailing addresses, not an e-mail address—you will not have access to computers.) You have studied the Core Values in this book and had them remediated by your Recruiter, so illegal drug use is not even on your radar any more, if it ever was.

Now it is time to ship out.

Last Preparations

Assemble these items:

A toothbrush
A proper form of identification
Any small religious items, such as your Bible
An address book, including at least two phone numbers and a
    home address for your next of kin
No more than $40 cash

You will not need anything else. The Marine Corps will provide you with everything from here forward. Be sure to tell your parents this. They should not send you hygiene items or clothing, underwear, etc. You are not going off to a college dormitory. Self-reliance is part of your training.

Get a good night's sleep the night before you ship out—it may be a while before you sleep again.

Don't dress like a bum, but there is no need to dress up either; the clothes you wear will be taken from you when you arrive. They will be stored and returned to you at the end—but they won't fit you any more. Besides, you will leave Recruit Training as a Marine, wearing your uniform.

Don't spend your money on a fresh haircut before you report, either; that will be taken care of soon.

Your Recruiter will transport you to MEPS, which is where you will ship from. You might be nervous, but pay attention to all his instructions—he will be reminding you of the items you need to bring and the items you should not have.

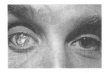

EYEBALLS! These are contraband items aboard the Recruit Depot—do not bring them.
Intoxicating beverages
Pornography or obscene literature
Subversive literature
Lewd or indecent pictures
Weapons of any kind or ammunition
Drugs or medicine of any kind
Gambling devices
Combustibles, lighters, matches
Prophylactics
Food, candy, gum
Tobacco of any kind
Battery or electrically operated devices

MEPS

At MEPS, Marines will go over your enlistment contract once again. Just like the first time, be certain that you understand it. If you are unsure, ask questions. This is not like the movies; the personnel at MEPS are there to help you. Be certain about what's in your contract. If your Recruiter promised you a specific job, ensure that you SEE that information in it. It is important that you make sure your contract says what you think it does—after all, you are giving your word to uphold everything in it.

Now you have reached the point where you will turn all the lessons from the previous 13 chapters into action.

The Oath of Enlistment: you will be sworn in again. The last time this happened, you were being sworn into the Delayed Entry Program. This time, you are being sworn into the active-duty United States Marine Corps. Pay attention to the words. You now

The Oath of Enlistment. You are sworn into
the active duty Marine Corps.

know what INTEGRITY and HONOR mean. When you swear the Oath, you are giving your word, committing the next eight years of your life to your new profession, the profession of arms. Your word is your bond.

MEPS personnel will then arrange transportation to the Marine Corps Recruit Depot. Remember "hurry up and wait." No need to get excited at this point; just relax—except for when you need to follow instructions.

MCRD

Your trip will culminate with a bus ride onto the Marine Corps Recruit Depot (MCRD). The bus pulls into Receiving Barracks and stops. A Drill Instructor steps onto the bus and begins to give instructions for you to follow. This will likely be the first REAL Drill Instructor you have seen. Your stress level will probably begin to rise rapidly.

Focus on two things:

1. Engage all of your senses to obtain and process information. Listen to instructions; look at (but not directly—use your peripheral vision) posted signs; observe the Drill Instructor's hand and arm motions; and feel the direction the rest of the group is moving.
2. Calm down. Consciously control your breathing to slow your heart rate, and focus on thinking clearly.

The ability to mentally process lots of information, lower your stress level, follow instructions, and make timely, calm decisions will be the key to success in Recruit Training. Not coincidentally, it will be the key to surviving on a battlefield, too.

The Yellow Footprints

You will be positioned on a set of yellow footprints and instructed in the basic drill position, the position of attention

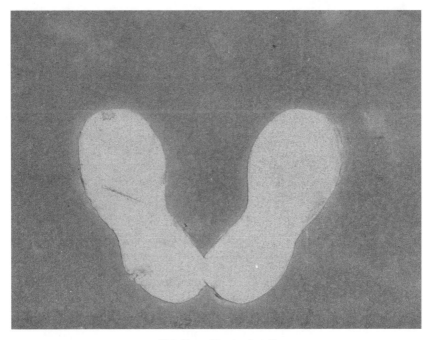

"Yellow Footprints"

When you get here, move fast, remain
calm and process information.

(POA). At this point, a Drill Instructor will be assaulting all of your senses with information. Remember to remain calm and process the information. Never disengage your brain and just become part of the herd. Much of the information being hurled at you should not be new to you—you already read it in this book.

A common phenomenon when confronted with the reality of your arrival at the Recruit Depot is an overwhelming flood of self-doubt. "Was it a mistake to do this?" This is common, in fact pervasive—almost everyone around you will be thinking the same thing. The difference is, YOU know this is a normal reaction. You also know this will quickly pass, often in a matter of minutes. Consciously force that self-doubt out of your head and get back to using all your senses to process information.

Arriving at Receiving Barracks

Receiving Barracks functions in an assembly-line process:

You will be checked for contraband (listed in the previous EYEBALLS! graphic).

You will be issued everything you need for Recruit Training. Be sure your family and friends know this and do not waste their money sending you items you do not need.

Your hair will be cut.

Your civilian clothes will be inventoried and boxed.

You will be issued a camouflage uniform, and you will put it on.

You will be issued other gear.

Within an hour you will go from a long-haired civilian to a bald, uniformed recruit.

Continually process information. When you are waiting in line, you may not be able to see, but you can open your ears and listen. Learn from everything you hear. Drill Instructors speak loudly, so you will always hear what they are saying. Listen to what is going on up ahead as Drill Instructors make corrections to other recruits—so you can learn from their corrections, too.

Within an hour of your arrival, you will be given the opportunity to make a brief phone call home. The purpose of this call is to notify your parents that you have arrived safely at MCRD, just as you would do when you reached your destination on any

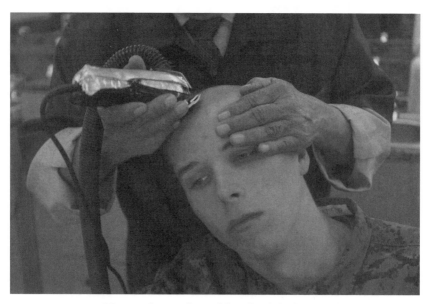

No need to arrive with a fresh haircut.
Within an hour everyone will get this one.
United States Marine Corps photo by Cpl. Matthew S. Lemieux

trip. Go ahead and tell them you are there and you are fine; don't worry them. Enjoy this short phone call—you won't get another one until you've earned it.

The Purpose of Receiving Barracks

The next few days will be full of basic instructions:

How to make your rack.
How to shave.
How to eat in the chow hall.
How to wear your uniform.
How to form basic drill formations.
…and a lot more.

As basic as these things sound, there is a lot to learn. As a Marine, all of these skills are taught for efficiency and functionality under any circumstance.

During your brief stay at Receiving Barracks, you will establish a bank account for your pay, and you will begin a service record book to record your military career, as well as medical and dental records. You will receive lots of shots/inoculations. A bit of advice: never look at the needles. Often these shots are delivered by a gun, one that is quite efficient and fast—but also designed with a stationary target in mind.

You will live in a large room, called a squad bay, with up to ninety of your fellow recruits. The collection of recruits in this room is your platoon. You will be with them throughout the entire training cycle, so start getting to know them. Do this by observation. Notice who appears to be having difficulty; they may need your help as training progresses. Notice who is fast; they can help you help others. You are going to be together for a long time, and are going to endure many hardships together. It is much easier to accomplish that as a team, so start forming that team now. Help others whenever you can. As soon as you accomplish any assigned task, help someone else who is not done. Begin to establish yourself as someone your platoon mates can count on. Others will see what you are doing, and begin to help others, too. You will have already begun to lead—by example.

An unseen enemy will already be attacking you. The recruits in your platoon come from all over the world, and when they arrive they are carrying germs from all those places with them. Together, you have created a germ stew, and it is now on every item you touch. Many recruits will get sick early in training. This will pass; all of you will begin developing your immunity immediately. But help yourself: keep your hands away from your face, unless instructed otherwise. Wash your hands whenever you are given the opportunity.

Quickly, you will settle into a routine at Receiving Barracks. The stress level is low, and there is no intensity to the training. The purpose of your stay here is mostly administrative. Most things you are taught are simply to sustain you until your real training begins. However, do not waste this time. Continue to prepare yourself for Recruit Training. Practice moving with a sense of urgency, practice assisting others, and do whatever things you are taught to the best of your ability. Start developing successful habits NOW. The Drill Instructors will be telling your fellow recruits who are moving slowly or not following instructions that things will be changing soon. This is an *understatement*.

Your time at Receiving Barracks will end in days. The members of your platoon will pack up everything they now possess into their seabags (large duffel bags). Your platoon will move to your training company barracks. This movement is called "the seabag drag" because it isn't pretty. It is also the last *easy* thing you will do in Recruit Training.

The training cycle is about to begin.

Training Tactics for Receiving Barracks

1. Use all of your senses to process information. Constantly increase your **KNOWLEDGE**.

2. Constantly remind yourself to mentally calm down, to slow down your breathing and lower your stress level. This will begin to build your **COURAGE**.

3. Always help others in your platoon. Develop an **UNSELFISH** attitude.

Chapter 15

Pick-Up and Forming

"The acceleration of a body is directly
proportional to the force applied."

—Sir Isaac Newton

Your seabag drag has come to an end. Your platoon has
"grounded your gear" (leaving your equipment in a designated
spot) in your new squad bay. It will be your platoon's home
throughout the first third of training. You, along with the rest of
your platoon, are herded onto the quarterdeck. You sit down facing
a closed hatch (door). Your Drill Instructors are on the other side,
and training is about to begin.

Right now, start using everything you've learned and practiced
about dealing with stress: concentrate on lowering your heart rate,
keeping your mind engaged, and using all your senses to process
information. And get ready to learn more, because information is

about to start coming at you at a high volume: in large amounts, at a high rate of speed.

Some Marines from your chain of command above your platoon level will briefly address your platoon. After this, you will only see these Marines occasionally. Your platoon's Drill Instructors will conduct your daily training, and you will see them *constantly*.

Now you meet them. The hatch bursts open. Your Senior Drill Instructor leads the others out. They move crisply and demonstrate purposefulness in their actions. The Senior Drill Instructor speaks. Training is about to commence, and he tells you what is expected of you. He also makes a commitment to you: the Drill Instructors' mission is to transform you into a United States Marine.

*   *   *

Training begins. You have just merged onto the freeway. You left the on-ramp at 25 mph, and the freeway is moving at 80 mph. You have to get up to speed. Or, if you are a dragster, imagine that the light just turned green. Everything moves faster than you can imagine. You might get the same feeling here as you did back on the "yellow footprints." As confused as you are, remember, so is everyone else. **Your goal is to try to learn as much as you can as fast as you can**. You will receive more information than anyone can process. This is intentional. It is your first real exposure to thinking under duress.

Remember the big picture. Your Drill Instructors are constantly testing and evaluating your COMMITMENT—nothing will be good enough for them. They are also developing your HONOR—do not turn on your fellow recruits. Slow ones need your help, not your anger. Your Drill Instructors bombard all of your senses to disorient you, to put you way out of any comfort zone. They are challenging your COURAGE. Develop it by forcing yourself to remain mentally calm during physical exertion and emotional stress. Simultaneously activate all of your senses to process information.

Drill Instructors make corrections loudly. Keep your ears
open and learn from corrections made on others.

During Pick-up and Forming, you are taught how to train. Everything here is a building block upon which more training will be stacked later. It is important to build a strong base. Everything has a precision to it. Even though you are not given the time to achieve that precision, know that "close" is not good enough—it will not be good enough on the battlefield when your fellow Marines are depending on you, and it isn't good enough now. Accomplish as much as you can when are given a task, and **move on when instructed to do so**. Your Drill Instructors will point out where you have fallen short. At this point in training, that will be *always*. The Drill Instructors will not point out these corrections to you politely. But do not get your feelings hurt, and do not take it as a personal attack. You are being told what you need to learn, so process the corrections.

In Pick-up and Forming, you are taught Basic Daily Routine (BDR). You no longer do anything by yourself. Everything a platoon does must be done efficiently so as to get the entire platoon through it quickly, to free up more time to train more. BDR is the procedure you will follow to start and end the training day. It is an

The M16A4 service rifle you are issued will be with you throughout
Recruit Training. Treat it well.
United States Marine Corps photo by Cpl. Matthew S. Lemieux

assembly-line procedure. If you become confused, use your senses
to perceive what the rest of your platoon is doing, and get on board!

In this phase, many of the basic daily functions you learned at
Receiving Barracks are taken to a new level of efficiency. You are
now in a training company, and things must move faster. Because
time is a precious commodity, you will receive training even when
you do not realize it. When you are seated on the quarterdeck, you
must sit in a very specific stance—the same stance from which you
will fire your rifle in a few weeks. When you hold your tray in the
chow hall, you will hold it with your forearms parallel to the deck
and your elbows tucked in to your sides—the same way you will
perform close order drill with your weapon.

What goes on in Pick-up and Forming may appear, from your
perspective, to be madness or chaos. It is in actuality quite
precisely scripted. Do not struggle against the system of

training—have faith in it! It has worked to train Marines to win our nation's battles since 1775, and it will work on you.

One of the highlights of Pick-up and Forming is the issuance of your M16A4 service rifle. If you are like I was, this will be the first rifle you have ever held. Even if it is not, treat it like it is, and listen to everything you are taught about it. Do not bring any bad habits with you. You will be taught by the best in the world; do not try to out-think them.

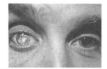 **EYEBALLS!** The characteristics of the M16A4 service rifle: it is a lightweight, magazine-fed, gas-operated, air-cooled, shoulder-fired weapon (LMGAS), capable of firing semi-automatically or in a three-round burst. Its max effective range is 550 meters for a point target and 800 meters for an area target.

Follow all instructions. Treat this rifle as if it is
the first weapon you have ever held. Do not
bring any bad habits with you.
United States Marine Corps photo by Cpl. Matthew S. Lemieux

A Drill Instructor demonstrates
the position of "Port Arms."
United States Marine Corps photo by Cpl. Matthew S. Lemieux

Despite your best efforts to keep your brain engaged, more information will be delivered to you than you can retain. Do not become alarmed. During the flood, you learned something that someone around you did not, and someone around you learned something you did not. *The strength of the Marine is The Corps, and the strength of The Corps is the Marine.* So help each other! Practice TEAMWORK.

Training Tactics for Pick-up and Forming

1. Start thinking of your platoon as your team.
2. Lead by example, not with your mouth.
3. Help others in your platoon whenever you can.
4. Do not worry about "why"; accept that everything happens for a reason.
5. Prioritize speed at this point; precision will come later.

6. Remember that nothing is personal in Recruit Training, regardless of how it seems.

7. Constantly focus on lowering your heart rate, staying mentally calm, and thinking clearly.

8. Use all your senses to process information—start turning your brain into a thinking machine that works under any circumstances.

One last piece of advice, from a former Drill Instructor: Realize that all recruits make mistakes—lots of them. You are learning an entirely new profession, and we throw information at you very fast. Accept that you will make mistakes. Don't take yourself too seriously.

At night after lights out in the squad bay, when it is finally quiet, think about something funny that happened during that training day. You won't have to think very hard. Have a quiet laugh.

Pick-up and Forming lasts four days. It is followed by First Phase.

Chapter 16

First Phase Training

"Share your courage with each other as
we enter the uncertain terrain."

—General James Mattis

As a recruit, you will not notice the transition from Pick-up and Forming into First Phase Training. From your perspective, it will be one continuous barrage of information, corrections, and disorienting experiences coming at you. You and the rest of your platoon will be kept constantly off balance and will never be able to get into any sort of comfort zone. The weaker-minded recruits in your platoon will begin to turn on the team. For others, the newness and excitement of change will turn into homesickness. For still others, self-doubt will creep in. The "Recruit Crud" sickness will hit many. If you are not feeling at a low point, rest assured that others around you are.

CLOSE-ORDER DRILL: The basic drill position of "Order Arms."
United States Marine Corps photo by Cpl. Matthew S. Lemieux

REMEMBER THAT ALL THIS IS BY DESIGN! The difference is, you know to expect this. You recognize why it is happening. You know the key to overcoming this adversity.

* * *

First Phase Training includes the following elements:

Close-Order Drill

This is the term given to marching and executing precision movements with your rifle. You will do a lot of this. If you have been taught any close-order drill prior to arriving at the Recruit Depot, *forget it!* Unless a Marine Drill Instructor taught it to you, it probably was instructed incorrectly.

PHYSICAL TRAINING: The techniques for negotiating obstacles are first taught and then demonstrated. Obstacles are 75% technique and 25% muscle.
United States Marine Corps photo by Cpl. Matthew S. Lemieux

PHYSICAL TRAINING: A Drill Instructor teaches the technique.
United States Marine Corps photo by Cpl. Matthew S. Lemieux

There are many reasons for performing close-order drill. It develops your confidence in handling your weapon and facilitates moving troops from place to place with military order. But that is all secondary; the primary reason for close-order drill is to instruct you in discipline and to instill instantaneous obedience to orders. These are critical building blocks of the profession of arms.

These lessons are abstractly taught, but are life-and-death important. For instance, if you lack the discipline to remain still and not adjust at the end of a drill movement, you will lack the discipline to remain still in an ambush position on a battlefield. The same skill set that is instilled by precision execution of a drill command is the same skill set necessary to quickly get your rifle into your shoulder, assume a good firing position, align the sights, and hit what you are shooting at. The intensity with which you perform rifle manual (the name given to rifle drill movements) is the same intensity (and the same muscle groups) with which you will execute a bayonet thrust.

Physical Training (PT)

This should not be surprising to you. Unless you signed up by accident, certainly you expected massive doses of PT in Recruit Training. The part you will not notice is that there is a scientific method to the PT schedule. It is designed to train different muscle groups on different days. It is structured for you to put out maximum effort on every exercise. Do not try to pace yourself—your Drill Instructors will not allow this anyway!

Pay attention to the instructions given on how to negotiate obstacles. Doing so successfully takes 75% technique and 25% muscle. The obstacles are designed for explosive muscle exertions—you cannot negotiate them timidly. Watch the instructors, have faith that the technique works, and ATTACK!

When running in formation, stay in step with the recruit in front of you and sound off to the Drill Instructor's cadence. Feed off the motivation and let the formation pull you along. Pay attention to

PHYSICAL TRAINING: A Drill Instructor
demonstates how to do an exercise.
United States Marine Corps photo by Cpl. Matthew S. Lemieux

PHYSICAL TRAINING: Recruits attack—
75% technique and 25% muscle.
United States Marine Corps photo by Cpl. Matthew S. Lemieux

the cadences. They are comical and motivating and will take your mind off the running.

PHYSICAL TRAINING: Top, formation run.
Bottom, building muscle and endurance is painful.
Push through the pain. It is temporary.
United States Marine Corps photos by Cpl. Matthew S. Lemieux

Building muscle and endurance is painful. When this pain begins to overwhelm you, remember that **the pain you are feeling is temporary, but the pride you will get from NOT quitting is forever**. Push through the pain. Your Drill Instructors will help you with this. You will discover that your limits were self-imposed. You are capable of far more than you realize.

Incentive Training (IT)

This is the part you may have seen in Hollywood movies: a Drill Instructor standing over a Recruit doing push-ups, etc. This training technique is employed when a recruit is having trouble with self-discipline. It is not pleasant, and it is not meant to be. When this happens to you—and it will—do not take it personally. Accept your punishment like the professional you are training to be, and **move on** when it is done.

Your Drill Instructors will make this seem very personal. They will say things to you during this that will sting—if you let it. Remember, everything here happens for a reason. The Drill Instructors are constantly testing your courage, honor, and commitment. The adversity you will face in the future on a battlefield can also seem very personal and spirit-crushing. Your Drill Instructors are preparing you to overcome that.

Nothing is personal on a battlefield; it just seems that way. The same is true for Recruit Training. Develop an armor plating for your heart. Do not let anything damage your motivation or crush your spirit. Take pride in your ability to do this. This mental toughness will serve you well in everything you do in life.

Classroom Instruction

You will receive numerous classes in the "House of Knowledge." You will be tired from training, so it will be easy to let your mind wander rather than pay attention to the instruction. Fight this. Remember, you are turning your brain into an all-weather, any-circumstance data processor that is unaffected by stress, duress, or fatigue.

Your classroom instruction will be on Marine Corps history, customs and courtesies, and first aid. Stay focused. When you are faced with real-life wounded, it will be too late to pull out a book and brush up on your knowledge. The profession of arms is serious business, not one to be undertaken halfway.

INCENTIVE TRAINING: Develop mental toughness.
Take corrections like a professional and don't
take anything personally.
United States Marine Corps photo by Cpl. Matthew S. Lemieux

CLASSROOM INSTRUCTION: Stay alert in class.
A Marine's mind is his best weapon.
United States Marine Corps photo by Cpl. Matthew S. Lemieux

CLASSROOM INSTRUCTION: A first aid training station.

Close Combat

In First Phase Training, you are introduced to the Marine Corps martial arts program and bayonet fighting. Pay close attention—all of the techniques you will be taught are amazingly effective, if executed correctly. They are based on the best martial arts techniques from around the world. You will learn about "muscle memory": you will repetitively rehearse techniques to the point that your body can execute them without conscious thought. Your body will be trained to reflexively perform. To get there, you must train through repetition. You will strike, strike, and strike some more. You will get struck and struck some more. You will throw and be thrown. You should get flight pay for all the time you will spend in the air! Remember, you are in the introductory stage. Focus on technique.

Swim Instruction

Marines are soldiers of the sea and serve on Navy ships. You must be able to swim. If you do not know how to swim, relax, you

CLOSE COMBAT: A basic throw. These techniques are repetitively
trained to develop "muscle memory."
United States Marine Corps photo by Cpl. Matthew S. Lemieux

will be taught by the best in the world. Recruits arrive at the Depot
with different skill levels, and everyone will be broken down into
appropriate ability groups and taught accordingly. The key is to
RELAX. You cannot fight the water, so do not try. Follow
instructions, learn the techniques, and you will float!

CLOSE COMBAT: Top, DI Gunny:
Drill Instructor Nick Popaditch
instills mental toughness with his recruits.
Bottom, You learn to throw another
and how to land when thrown.

CLOSE COMBAT: Top, you must be able to fight your
way out of a bad situation. Bottom, pugil sticks are used to simulate
and train bayonet fighting.

So will your pack and rifle. Your pack is quite buoyant, and your rifle will rest on it. It is actually quite amazing. You will be able to jump into the water with a pack and rifle and quickly turn yourself into a mobile gunboat. You will turn your cammies into floatation devices that actually work. Using these techniques, Marines have stayed alive for days while adrift in the open ocean.

* * *

Everything in First Phase Training is building the foundation. Part of building the foundation is breaking down the parts. This is both painful and frustrating. Often you will feel weaker than you did when you arrived, and you will frequently feel less intelligent.

The physical portion is easy to figure out: your body is being broken down to be built up, so it is fatigued.

The mental portion is less obvious. You are constantly being put under stress and then forced to make quick, often instantaneous

SWIMMING: Recruits arrive with different swimming skill levels. Even if you arrive with no ability whatsoever, you will be taught how to survive in the water.

United States Marine Corps photo by Cpl. Matthew S. Lemieux

SWIMMING: Do not fight the water and you will float.

decisions. Prior to Recruit Training, you never learned under these circumstances, but your mind **must** learn to function like this. The ability to make quick, accurate decisions under duress is the key to survival and victory on a battlefield.

Remember the win-win scenario. Once you learn to think in this manner, you will be ahead of your peers for the rest of your life.

Training Tactics for First Phase Training

1. Constantly focus on controlling your breathing to lower your heart rate. This will help you think clearly.
2. Activate all your senses to process information around you. Turn your brain into an all-weather, any-environment data processor.
3. No matter how tired you are, do not quit, physically or mentally.
4. Listen to corrections made on other recruits. Drill Instructors make these loud so all of you can hear them.

SWIMMING: The "Tank"

SWIMMING: Part of your swim qualification is a leap
off the high tower to simulate jumping from
the side of a ship, so jump...

They are expecting all of you to learn from corrections
made on individuals.

5. Help other recruits whenever you can. Teamwork is the
   key to success. The Drill Instructors will set the
   conditions so that it is easiest to function as an
   individual—just to test your commitment and honor.

6. Do not worry about any "whys" at this point. None of
   them will be obvious. Have faith that everything that is
   happening is designed to make you better in some way.
   Put out maximum effort on any task.

7. Do not try to pace yourself, despite your fatigue. The
   Drill Instructors are on the lookout for this and will get

that last bit of effort out of you. The training program will not work to its best effect if you are not fatigued.

8. Do not get frustrated, even though First Phase is structured to frustrate you. Learn as much as you can, as fast as you can, and KEEP MOVING FORWARD!

I decided to stick in one Drill Instructor secret at the end of this chapter, to reward you for making the effort to study this book. Here it is:

Pugil sticks are padded sticks used to simulate bayonet fighting. When pugil stick fighting: on the whistle, quickly and violently strike with a bayonet thrust to your opponent's face—basically, make a quick jab to the face, but step into it. This is a very easy technique to execute. Your opponent, a basically trained recruit, will not have the skill level to parry it. You should get a quick victory, and possibly a brief rest.

...and enjoy the ride down.

BAYONET THRUST: Win here and you may enjoy a brief rest.

Chapter 17

Second Phase Training

"You don't hurt 'em if you don't hit 'em."

—Lieutenant General Lewis "Chesty" Puller

This phase of Recruit Training consists of rifle range and field training.

Marksmanship is the hallmark of Marines, and Second Phase is where you learn it. By now you will have been carrying your rifle for three weeks. During drill that 8.75-pound rifle has felt like it weighed 100 pounds. In pugil stick fighting, you learned how to kill with it. During Second Phase, you get to fire that rifle—a lot.

During Second Phase you live at the rifle range. The evening BDR will incorporate a new step: reciting the *Rifleman's Creed* before you hit the rack at night.

You have drilled with it. In Second Phase
you finally get to fire your rifle.
United States Marine Corps photo by Cpl. Matthew S. Lemieux

RIFLEMAN'S CREED

This is my rifle. There are many like it, but this one is mine. My rifle is my best friend. It is my life. I must master it as I master my life. My rifle, without me, is useless. Without my rifle, I am useless. I must fire my rifle true. I must shoot straighter than any enemy who is trying to kill me. I must shoot him before he shoots me. I will. . . .

My rifle and myself know that what counts in this war is not the rounds we fire, the noise of our burst, nor the smoke we make. We know that it is the hits that count. We will hit. . .

My rifle is human, even as I, because it is my life. Thus, I will learn it as a brother. I will learn its weakness, its strength, its parts, its accessories, its sights and its barrel. I will keep my rifle clean and ready, even as I am clean and ready. We will become part of each other. We will. . .

Before God I swear this creed. My rifle and myself are the defenders of my country. We are the masters of our enemy. We are the saviors of my life. So be it, until victory is America's and there is no enemy, but Peace.

In the Marine Corps, every Marine is a rifleman first, regardless of his or her military specialty. Your worth as a Marine is directly tied to your ability to master marksmanship. This is the most critical skill you will acquire as a United States Marine. The greatest tactics ever devised are useless if, at the critical moment of engagement, you cannot hit the enemy.

You didn't know it, but your Drill Instructors have been preparing you for success in Second Phase ever since you arrived at the Depot.

The following are some aspects of Second Phase marksmanship training:

GRASS WEEK: Primary Marksmanship Instructor
(PMI) teaching fundamentals.
United States Marine Corps photo by Cpl. Matthew S. Lemieux

Grass Week

Your marksmanship instruction begins with Grass Week. During this week, you are taught the Marine Corps firing positions of standing, sitting, kneeling, and prone.

Mastery of these positions facilitates a Marine being able to attain a stabilized firing platform, under any circumstance and on any terrain. Firing a rifle in combat is significantly different from movie depictions. Hollywood always shows standing or running shooters spraying showers of bullets at the enemy while simultaneously shouting epithets or profanity at them. The reality is that most shots are single, well-aimed rounds fired by a stable shooter from far out of vocal range. Grass Week is where you begin to learn how to do this.

You are taught by a Primary Marksmanship Instructor (PMI), and you will spend most of Grass Week with him. This Marine is not a Drill Instructor. He teaches all aspects of Marine Corps marksmanship. Marksmanship is the hallmark of Marines. We are the best shooters in the world, and the PMIs are the best of the best.

As was the case with close-order drill, whatever shooting knowledge you arrived with, **FORGET IT!** During my time as a Drill Instructor, I saw that recruits who never fired a weapon before in their lives, almost without exception, out-shot recruits who grew up firing rifles and pistols. Whatever shooting experience you arrive with is probably permeated with bad habits. Marksmanship is built on solid fundamentals and discipline.

The PMI will teach you the basic firing positions. These rely on skeletal stability and muscle relaxation. The first thing you will notice is that they bear similarity to how you were forced to sit in classrooms during First Phase Training. The next thing you will notice is that the positions become quite uncomfortable after just a short period. This is cured on the "circles." The circles are round, cement sidewalks that simulate the firing line on the rifle range. You will spend extended periods in the different firing positions to train your body to contort into them and achieve the comfort level to get muscle relaxation and obtain a "natural point of aim" for you and your weapon.

Do not try to out-think anything you are taught. It works, but only if you do it the way you are instructed. Be disciplined. The shooting positions are uncomfortable, but if you work hard during Grass Week, they will become natural for you. The reverse is true

GRASS WEEK: Recruits in the sitting firing
position on the "circles."
United States Marine Corps photo by Cpl. Matthew S. Lemieux

GRASS WEEK: Standing firing position. This is the least stable of all firing positions, yet the most popular in the movies.
United States Marine Corps photo by Cpl. Matthew S. Lemieux

as well: if you "sandbag" during Grass Week, you will struggle during Firing Week.

GRASS WEEK: The most stable firing position is the prone position.
United States Marine Corps photo by Cpl. Matthew S. Lemieux

Firing Week

This week is just what its name implies: you will fire your rifle on the rifle range. Success on the range is built on hard work during Grass Week. Firing Week requires discipline and faith. Discipline will keep you in a good firing position, and faith will be required to hit the target. How is this?

During Grass Week, you were instructed to focus your eyesight on the front sight tip of your rifle (the raised sight near the muzzle

FIRING WEEK: Your PMI will continue to
instruct you during Firing Week.
United States Marine Corps photo by Cpl. Matthew S. Lemieux

end of your rifle). This is critical in order to properly align your
rifle sights. Since your eye can only focus on one thing, this will
mean the target you are shooting at will be blurry, especially the
500-meter targets. You must have faith that this works—and it
does. If you don't, and focus on the target instead of your sights, it
will make you feel better when you squeeze the trigger—but you

FIRING WEEK: Marksmanship that has been developed since the
days of sharpshooters in ship's riggings is taught to you.
United States Marine Corps photo by Cpl. Matthew S. Lemieux

will never hit the target, because your rifle's sights will not be aligned.

At the range, your platoon will be divided in half. Some will fire on the morning relay while the other half works in the "pits." The pits or "butts" are down-range where the targets are located. There you pull targets down behind a parapet after they are shot at and mark where they were hit. All firing evolutions are timed. If you work slowly here, the firing recruit is poorly served and disadvantaged. By this point in training, teamwork should be common; but if it is not, be a leader in the pits and demand it from your fellow recruits. Of course, the best leadership demonstrates by example.

You will fire the entire qualification course on Monday through Thursday of Firing Week. Thursday is referred to as Pre-Qual. It is conducted as an exact replica of Friday, Qualification Day.

FIRING WEEK: Top, just as the camera cannot focus on the rifle's sights and the target at the same time, neither can your eye. You must focus on the sights. The target will be blurry, as it is here, but you will hit it. Bottom, on the rifle range your platoon is divided into firing relays. Half will be firing and half are working in the target "pits."

United States Marine Corps photos by Cpl. Matthew S. Lemieux

Qualification Day

On the Friday of Firing Week, you will shoot for score. You must qualify with your rifle on this day or you will be recycled back in training to Grass Week. This is your first real test of mental toughness. You have been trained for this, so you will possess all the skills to pass—but can you perform when called upon?

Be confident. You have been practicing to engage your brain calmly and efficiently under stress. Now is time to prove it. If you make a bad shot, learn from it and move on. Remember, the only shot you can positively change is the one you are about to take.

There are bigger principles involved here than your rifle score:

- Can you overcome a mistake you might make? Marines must be able to move on and perform afterwards.

QUALIFICATION DAY: You cannot get the round back after you fire it. If you make a bad shot, put it behind you and focus on the shot you are about to take.

United States Marine Corps photo by Cpl. Matthew S. Lemieux

QUALIFICATION DAY: This is a test of your ability
to execute skills you are taught.
United States Marine Corps photo by Cpl. Matthew S. Lemieux

- Can you perform skills you are taught, upon command, under stress?
- Can you hit a designated target quickly and accurately upon command? On a battlefield, your enemy will be trying to hit you, your fellow Marines, or innocents. Are you able to execute marksmanship more efficiently than your enemy? Remember *The Rifleman's Creed.*

QUALIFICATION DAY: You must be able to execute
this skill better than your enemy.
United States Marine Corps photo by Cpl. Matthew S. Lemieux

Hikes

Concurrent with marksmanship training, your platoon will go on two hikes. These are to familiarize you with forced marches, called "humps." During these, your platoon will move across broken terrain in two columns with rifles and field gear. The speed will be slightly faster than marching, but slower than running. This

HIKES: A hike tests teamwork.

sounds simple, and in theory it is. In practice, these can be difficult. Most important, these hikes test teamwork.

You will have an opportunity to prep your gear. Secure your uniform and gear well. Anything that is loose will rub, and when something is rubbing on every step, it will wear a hole in you within miles. Once your gear is ready, help someone else. Check each other for anything overlooked.

The formation will move at a steady pace that doesn't slow. Keep a tight interval. Do not drift back from the recruit in front of you. Whenever you drift back, you will have to run to catch up. And if you fall back up front, recruits in the back will have to run to catch up an interval that you did not maintain.

Hikes are a steady source of discomfort. Do not focus on it. Sound off cadences, keep your interval tight, and help others to keep your mind from focusing on the unpleasantness.

FIELD WEEK: Camouflage skills are taught during Field Week.
United States Marine Corps photo by Cpl. Matthew S. Lemieux

Field Week

Field Week training is probably what you envisioned when you thought about joining the Marines. This is the crawling-through-mud and firing-your-weapon-at-moving-targets type stuff. If you do not enjoy this sort of training, you are in the wrong profession.

You will be instructed how to move across terrain tactically, both day and night. Be aware, especially at night—everything is training.

Here is another Drill Instructor secret, a reward for taking the initiative to read this book: during night infiltration courses, Drill Instructors will sneak into your ranks, looking like recruits. They will speak to you and attempt to convince you to do un-tactical things. When this happens, tell the voice in the dark to shut up and

FIELD WEEK: After you have qualified on the rifle range, you will learn to apply marksmanship skills in more realistic scenarios.
United States Marine Corps photo by Cpl. Matthew S. Lemieux

stop giving your position away. You should do this to anyone—but in this case, you get to correct your Drill Instructors, for a change!

Field Week is a great opportunity to let your leadership and individual talents out. While your platoon is executing courses, it is easy to go through as an individual. Don't do it! It does not do you or your unit any good to get to the objective *by yourself*. Set the example by helping others who are slower than you. Always focus on WE, not I. Think of your unit as a wolfpack—it is much more effective as a team. Think of your enemy as jackals. They are always looking to pick off stragglers and individuals. Be a leader. Simply do not allow fellow recruits to act as individuals, and help stragglers who do not possess your talents. Practice being your brother's keeper until it becomes second nature to think of others ahead of yourself. Remember the win-win scenario. This habit will make you a good Marine and lead to a fulfilling, worthy life after The Corps.

During Field Week you will return to the rifle range and fire your weapon under more adverse circumstances. These challenges are designed for you to apply the marksmanship you learned in more realistic scenarios. Any time you fire your weapon, remember this: **engage your brain before you engage with your**

FIELD WEEK: Each Recruit carries half of one of these tents (called a shelter-half). The longer it takes to set these up, the less sleep you will get.
United States Marine Corps photo by Cpl. Matthew S. Lemieux

weapon. Make certain that your brain is fully operational when your rifle goes into your shoulder.

There are no squadbays during Field Week. Your platoon sleeps under the stars, rain or shine. You will get dirty, muddy, tired, motivated, challenged, and trained. You will start feeling more competent and less confused. You will think of your platoon's success more than your own. You are starting to know your fellow recruits quite well, and you are all learning how to work together to accomplish tasks. You are starting to transform into a Marine—probably without even realizing it.

Team Week/Interior Guard

Following Field Week, your platoon will be assigned to perform some maintenance function on the base. The name given to this week may seem a bit misleading. This will be the first time in Recruit Training that you are going to work independently, in smaller groups, and sometimes alone—without a Drill Instructor directly supervising you. How is this "Team" Week?

By this point, your Recruit Training is over halfway complete. The question you will answer during this week is: have you developed self-discipline, or do you still require forced discipline? If you still seek to loaf instead of work, you are a hindrance to your team. If you still require supervision to stay focused and on task, you are taking assets away from your team. However, if you have developed your discipline so that you can work independently, you are an asset to your team. If you have developed your leadership so that you can and will direct other recruits, you are an asset to your team. If you have improved your initiative to solve problems as they arise, without the need for additional orders, you are an asset to your team.

Perhaps the week would be better named Team Week *with a question mark after it.*

FIELD WEEK: Confusion is now being replaced by confidence.
United States Marine Corps photo by Cpl. Matthew S. Lemieux

Training Tactics for Second Phase Training

1. Do the work during Grass Week to be successful on Firing Week. Stay in your firing positions even though they are painful. There is no way during Firing Week to make up for failure to do this.

2. Ask questions during instruction from your PMI. Marksmanship is the most important skill you learn in Recruit Training. It is vitally important you understand it.

3. Start inspecting others' gear and equipment after you have inspected your own. Encourage others to do this. That is how Marine units prepare—by checking each other.

4. Once you have fired a round, realize you cannot get it back. Treat it as gone, and focus on your next shot.

5. The breathing you have been practicing to lower your heart rate will now be taught by your PMI and expected while firing. This one should be natural for you by now.

6. Do not waste time on the firing line, and do not rush. Make your actions deliberate.

7. Put safety at the front of your mind. You are now handling loaded weapons.

"The 0400 Marine"

When I was a young Marine, a noncommissioned officer told me about "the 0400 Marine." He told me that motivation, discipline, Core Values, and Semper Fi are easy in the middle of a sunshiny day. The real Marine, he continued, is the one who is motivated, displays Core Values, and believes in Semper Fi at 0400 (4 a.m.), when he is tired and cold and up against adversity. The Marine who is disciplined then, when no one else is looking . . . *that* is the real Marine—the "0400 Marine."

Chapter 18

Third Phase Training

"Lead me, follow me, or get out of my way."
—General George Patton

Third Phase Training is not quite the home stretch, but it is close to the end. More importantly, when you get to this point you will be acting more like a Marine and less like a recruit.

Third Phase Training is similar to First Phase Training, just more advanced. If First Phase took you through the high school versions of various training elements, Third Phase represents the college versions. Everything is both more detailed and done faster. This may sound somewhat reassuring, but Recruit Training is not about comfort zones. Your Drill Instructors will up the ante and demand more of you—a lot more!

Close-Order Drill

Your platoon has been taught all drill movements and will be looking sharp. Not only is your individual performance expected to be precise, but your platoon is now expected to succeed as a team. Your mistakes will be minor at this point, but will be treated as catastrophic. That is because Close-Order Drill is only partially about drill; more importantly, it is a training tool for much bigger concepts. Attention to detail in drill transfers to combat, such as properly aligning your sights when firing your rifle. Messing up in drill will earn you Incentive Training; but mess up with your rifle on a battlefield and the consequences are much more grievous. Therefore, Close-Order Drill is treated with the same seriousness.

During Third Phase Training, your platoon will be evaluated in drill. Be proud and shine. Your platoon will march on the parade deck alone, looking like Marines. Your Senior Drill Instructor's cadence will echo through the Depot. Although your Drill Instructors will not tell you this, they will be proud of you. But at this point, that is inconsequential. Pride and self-discipline will be driving you now, not fear of your Drill Instructors.

Physical Training (PT)

In First Phase Training, your body was broken down, constantly fatigued, and weak-feeling. In Third Phase, the build-up has begun. You will return to the obstacle courses, only this time you will run them twice, with less effort. Of course, Recruit Training is not about comfort zones—in fact, it actively prevents them—so more will now be expected. You will be pushed harder physically. Do not pace yourself—the training is designed for maximum output. Every pain you feel is building strength and stamina.

Formation runs will now look more like formations; your training company will be less strung out. Your platoon can now stay in step and knows how to sound off the cadences. Your company, running all in step and booming a cadence, will sound

You will have many opportunities to attack the Obstacle Course.

like a loudly beating drum—rolling thunder. Feed off this, using it for motivation.

Your courage and confidence will be tested on the high obstacles and the rappelling tower. These activities are probably the sort of training you envisioned when you pictured yourself as a Marine. The high obstacles are *visually* frightening, designed to scare you and test your courage and confidence, not your physical ability. All of the Recruits in your platoon have the physical ability to negotiate them, and you need to have confidence in your

The high obstacles test your courage.

The Rappel Tower

physical ability to leap when you are required to. If you lack the courage to leap with all your effort, you will not make it. By this point in training, you should be accustomed to facing fear. So ATTACK.

You will be evaluated on your physical fitness during Third Phase. You will take these tests simultaneously with the other recruits in your training company. Use this to improve your personal score. When running, pick out a recruit ahead of you and try to reel him in and pass him. After you have passed him, pick another and work your way to the front.

Close Combat

Marine Corps martial arts training will also move into the advanced stage: more strikes, more throws, more getting struck, and more getting thrown. Your confusion will be replaced with knowledge. The effectiveness of the techniques will probably surprise you. You will be tested on your knowledge, and will leave Recruit Training with your first belt—a Tan belt. Marine Corps martial arts will be part of your Marine Corps life for your entire enlistment. You will have the opportunity to work your way up to a Black belt.

Third Phase incorporates more bayonet training. You will fight with pugil sticks in the "Thunderdome" and "the Bridge Over Troubled Waters." At the Thunderdome you charge down a ramp into a room. Another recruit is doing the same from the opposite direction. Do not stop at the entrance and do not think of the other recruit as your teammate. Continue to charge into the unknown (COURAGE), spot your target (the other recruit), and ATTACK. By Third Phase, your mind will have learned to think under duress and should be able to sharply focus on delivering killing blows with your pugil stick. At the Bridge Over Troubled Waters you will pugil stick fight another recruit on a narrow bridge over a pool of water. Balance is key. Focus on stepping into every strike. This will force your opponent off balance. Then finish him with a killing blow. The recruit who remains on the bridge is the victor.

Prac-Test

You will be evaluated on the knowledge taught during Recruit Training. Recruits are evaluated in two ways, by written test and PracAp (a physical demonstration of skills). The written test is similar to any multiple choice test you have ever taken. Do not leave any answers blank—guess, if necessary—because you are credited with any correct answers and not penalized for incorrect ones. You can begin preparing for this test NOW by mastering the knowledge in Chapters 6-12 of this book.

All through training, you have been teaching your mind to think clearly when called upon. Here is an opportunity to prove it. Marines are *thinkers*—the best in the world.

*   *   *

In Third Phase Training your hair is allowed to grow out a little on top and your body is starting to sprout muscles. You are starting to look like a Marine. More importantly, you are starting to think like one.

If you have not turned your individual talents loose yet, WHAT ARE YOU WAITING FOR? If you are smart, tutor other recruits during "square away time." If you are strong, take the heavier loads. If you are fast, quickly finish tasks and then assist others who are slower.

Always look for ways to make your team (platoon) more effective. Divide assigned tasks into parts and divide labor to accomplish it. Outgrow your Drill Instructors. Prove to them that you no longer need to be spoon-fed instructions. Self-discipline should be the norm—by this point, forced discipline from your Drill Instructors should be shameful to you.

Training Tactics for Third Phase Training

1. Everything in Third Phase is designed for you to think your way through. Make calm, clear decisions regardless of the chaos around you.

2. If you have not opened your mouth in Recruit Training, now is the time. Seek to contribute your talents and Lead. Become actively involved in solving problems.

3. Always seek to solve problems as a team. Divide tasks into smaller parts and assign recruits to each part, like on an assembly line. A Recruit Training platoon has many bodies and minds—utilize them all.

4. Know you have the physical ability to accomplish the high obstacles. Have the courage to confidently execute them. Leap when called upon to leap. You WILL make it.

5. Push yourself to maximum effort in PT. The training is not effective if you pace yourself. This is the building phase.

6. Do not rest on the Physical Fitness Test (PFT). Resting only fatigues you more. To achieve your max score, ATTACK—to the point of muscle failure.

7. Study your knowledge during "square away time."

8. Always put your platoon ahead of yourself. Your HONOR and COMMITMENT are always being evaluated. Furthermore, nothing in Recruit Training can be accomplished alone. Platoons comprised of selfish individuals always fail, and suffer greatly. Your Drill Instructors will apply as much pain as it takes to teach this vital lesson.

9. By this point, you should recognize that anytime you feel stressed, it is due to your own shortcomings. Lower your breathing and calm your mind (regardless of the physical surroundings or chaos around you) and force yourself to make clear, calm decisions.

"A Message to Garcia"

During the Spanish-American War, President McKinley wrote a letter to Cuban insurgent General Calixco Garcia requesting military intelligence. The letter was dispatched to Lieutenant Andrew Rowan, U.S. Army, in Washington, D.C., with the simple instruction, "Get that message to Garcia."

Lieutenant Rowan had no idea where in Cuba General Garcia was, but he had his mission and he set out to accomplish it. Lieutenant Rowan crossed an ocean, landed behind enemy lines, linked up with Cuban resistance fighters, and delivered the message to Garcia.

General Garcia then dispatched a message of his own in reply to the American President's. Lieutenant Rowan realized it was of vital importance to the success of the entire war. He again crossed enemy lines and an ocean and delivered the message from Garcia.

Lieutenant Rowan's example is the benchmark of military character. He had a mission but almost no details of how to accomplish it. He displayed COURAGE and COMMITMENT to stay on task and INITIATIVE to realize what needed to be done and then do it, without needing further orders. It is exactly that ability to think through problems that the Marine Corps seeks to instill in recruits—so much so that the phrase "Message to Garcia" is synonymous with initiative and mission accomplishment to Marines.

Chapter 19

The Crucible

"Uncommon valor was a common virtue."
—Admiral Chester Nimitz' assessment of Marines on Iwo Jima

    Much as a crucible takes molten steel and shapes it into a solid form, the "Crucible" will take everything you have learned in Recruit Training and bring it all together. This two and a half day training evolution is both mentally and physically challenging. Its purpose is to forge the physical and mental traits you have been taught into a tangible Marine character. It is the culmination of your training.

    In an industrial crucible, if substandard material is put in, weak steel is the product. The same is true here: if you have paced yourself throughout training, if you have not put the effort in, nothing "magical" is going to happen during the Crucible, and a

The Crucible brings the different parts together
to make a stronger whole.
United States Marine Corps photo by Cpl. Matthew S. Lemieux

weak product will come out the other side. However, if you have applied yourself in Recruit Training and pushed yourself throughout, something *will* happen here: the parts will be forged into a whole, and the whole will be greater than the sum of the parts.

*   *   *

Food and Sleep Deprivation

You have been training to think while under physical duress. The Crucible will make you prove it.

You will execute the entire training evolution on less than one day's ration. You will get only four hours' sleep per night. This combination puts your body in a state of physical stress that tests your stamina and challenges your mental capacity.

Physical Exhaustion

The Crucible is 54 miles long—you will be covering a lot of ground. You will be constantly challenged with mobility obstacles. You will be loaded down with gear. All this will be physically grueling.

Physical exhaustion, combined with food and sleep deprivation, is designed to shut your mind down. Fight this. Remember, you have turned your mind into an all-weather data processor that is impervious to fatigue.

Conduct of the Crucible

You will execute the Crucible as a squad of recruits (approximately 12-20) with a Drill Instructor. On the Crucible the Drill Instructor assumes a different role: he is a guide and evaluator. Recruits will make all leadership decisions, and will face the consequences of their actions, good as well as bad. Bad decisions will have repercussions.

The Crucible's 54-mile course is not flat.
United States Marine Corps photo by Cpl. Matthew S. Lemieux

Crucible Stations

You will continually be presented with challenges along the course. Your squad will be briefed on the situation and given a mission, with an established time limit. One recruit will be designated as the squad leader. The decisions are yours—the Drill Instructor will intervene only to prevent a safety hazard.

You and the other recruits will not be able to accomplish these missions as individuals, yet you cannot accomplish them without team members using their individual talents. Collectively all of you must be a team, and *you* as an individual must contribute your talents to the team. Finally, you cannot accomplish these missions without effective leadership—the leader must lead.

When the Crucible puts an obstacle in your path,
your team will go up and over it.
United States Marine Corps photo by Cpl. Matthew S. Lemieux

Fight physical exhaustion and never disengage your brain. Be a
thinker. Marines are the best thinkers in the world.
United States Marine Corps photo by Cpl. Matthew S. Lemieux

Eagle, Globe, and Anchor Ceremony

The Crucible will conclude with a long hike. Squads will
re-form into a platoon and the platoons will be re-assembled back
into a training company. Stay together and do not string out. Hike
as a unit—finish as a team.

The hike concludes with a ceremony. Your Drill Instructors
will award you your Eagle, Globe, and Anchor emblem. The Eagle,
Globe, and Anchor is the Marine Corps symbol. Marines have
worn it since 1868. The Marines who fought at Belleau Wood and
Iwo Jima carried this same symbol, and now you will have earned
yours, as well as your place in their ranks.

When your Drill Instructor puts your Eagle, Globe, and Anchor
in your hand, you will know who you are. Remember the wave of
self-doubt that hit you on the Yellow Footprints at Receiving
Barracks? At this ceremony, a wave of pride and self-confidence
will hit you instead. You will know you are different
now—changed forever.

Training Tactics for Success on the Crucible

1. Hydrate. Continue to drink water throughout the Crucible. You will rapidly dehydrate otherwise.

2. Pace out your food rations. Eat in small portions to make your food last, and to get the maximum energy from each item eaten.

3. Do not discard the salt and sugar packets in the rations. Mix those with water to make "Recruit Gatorade." This mixture will give you energy and help your body stay hydrated.

4. The challenge is more mental than physical. Force yourself to stay focused. Never just mentally drift into being one of the herd. Lead!

5. When in charge, TAKE CHARGE! Don't be afraid to make decisions. The only unacceptable mistake is a failure to act.

6. Prove you can follow orders from others as well as lead. This is Leadership (by example) also.

7. Don't expect—INSPECT. Constantly inspect your gear and the gear of those in your squad for items that have become loose or broken. This must become a constant habit.

8. Take care of your feet. Take off your boots and socks to air your feet out, and change your socks every chance you get. Failure to do this will render you unable to walk by the end of the Crucible's 54 miles. You will see this in others by the end.

9. Everything on the Crucible must be undertaken as a team. If *you* are performing any task alone, you are *wrong*.

Many Crucible Stations are named for Medal of Honor recipients. One of these is Corporal James Day. He was awarded the Medal of Honor for service as set forth in the following citation:

Citation
Day, James L.

"For conspicuous gallantry and intrepidity at the risk of his life above and beyond the call of duty as a squad leader serving with the Second Battalion, Twenty-Second Marines, Sixth Marine Division, in sustained combat operations against Japanese forces on Okinawa, Ryukya Islands from 14 to 17 May 1945.

On the first day, Corporal Day rallied his squad and the remnants of another unit and led them to a critical position forward of the front lines of Sugar Loaf Hill. Soon thereafter, they came under an intense mortar and artillery barrage that was quickly followed by a ferocious ground attack by some forty Japanese soldiers. Despite the loss of one-half of his men, Corporal Day remained at the forefront, shouting encouragement, hurling hand grenades, and directing deadly fire, thereby repelling the determined enemy. Reinforced by six men, he led his squad in repelling three fierce night attacks but suffered five additional Marines killed and one wounded, whom he assisted to safety.

Upon hearing nearby calls for corpsman assistance, Corporal Day braved heavy enemy fire to escort four seriously wounded Marines, one at a time, to safety. Corporal Day then manned a light machine gun, assisted by a wounded Marine, and halted another night attack. In the ferocious action, his machine gun was destroyed, and he suffered multiple white phosphorous and fragmentation wounds. He reorganized his defensive position in time to halt a fifth enemy attack with devastating small arms fire. On three separate occasions, Japanese soldiers closed to within a few feet of his foxhole, but were killed by Corporal Day.

During the second day, the enemy conducted numerous unsuccessful swarming attacks against his exposed position. When the attacks momentarily subsided, over 70 enemy dead were counted around his position. On the third day, a wounded and exhausted Corporal Day repulsed the enemy's final attack, killing a dozen enemy soldiers at close range. Having yielded no ground and with more than 100 enemy dead around his position, Corporal Day preserved the lives of his fellow Marines and made a significant contribution to the success of the Okinawa campaign.

By his extraordinary heroism, repeated acts of valor, and quintessential battlefield leadership, Corporal Day inspired the efforts of his outnumbered Marines to defeat a much larger enemy force, reflecting great credit upon himself and upholding the highest traditions of the Marine Corps and the United States Naval Service."

The Crucible Station named after Corporal Day takes approximately ten minutes to execute and is designed to simulate ten minutes of his experience on Sugar Loaf Hill, Okinawa. When you finish it you will be exhausted. Day did that for *two and a half days*—the same amount of time as the *entire* Crucible.

The character Corporal Day displayed has been passed down and taught to you. You are now brothers, and you have the responsibility of carrying The Corps' honor forward.

Chapter 20

Graduation

"Far better it is to dare mighty things, to win glorious
triumphs even though checkered by failure,
than to rank with those poor spirits who neither enjoy
nor suffer much because they live in the gray twilight
that knows neither victory nor defeat."

—President Theodore Roosevelt

The last week of Recruit Training is called Transition Week. It is just that: you are leaving behind the identity of a recruit and stepping up to a new one.

Do not think of this as a finish line, because it is not. You have reached the *starting* line.

*   *   *

Transition Week has a few key events:

Battalion Commander's Inspection

The Commanding Officer of your Recruit Training Battalion will inspect your training company. You will wear your service "A" uniform complete with your recently earned Eagle, Globe, and Anchor emblems. The inspecting officer will check your uniform and weapon for serviceability and cleanliness.

But that isn't the point. YOU are being inspected—your character, not the equipment on your body. During this inspection, you stand face-to-face with a Marine officer. Your Commanding Officer is inspecting your ability to display the Core Values and Leadership traits confidently. Demonstrate that you belong here. Display that you are ready to move on to the Fleet Marine Force.

Administration

You are assigned your Military Occupational Specialty (MOS). This is the job you will perform out in the Fleet Marine Force. (Remember, every Marine is a rifleman first.) If you contracted for a specific job, your assignment should match. If you came in on what is referred to as an "open contract" (no specific MOS), you are assigned one. Often this has already been accomplished. You receive your official orders to your next assignment. That will be a Marine formal school for further training.

You are authorized 10 days leave prior to reporting to your next assignment. Travel arrangements are finalized during this week.

Graduation Events

The graduating company will go on a motivation run around the Depot. This is for just that, motivation—and not just yours. Depot employees, Marines, families, and visitors come out to see our Corps' newest.

Your training company will receive a few hours of liberty call. You are not allowed to leave the Depot. Demonstrate the self-discipline and Core Values you have learned. Conduct yourself in a manner representative of the Corps. In all my time as a Drill Instructor, I never had a recruit who violated this. If you have family or friends visiting to see you graduate, you can spend this liberty time visiting with them.

Graduation Parade

The graduation parade is steeped in tradition. Every portion of it has a historical significance. The grandstands will be full of families, friends, and Marines. They are there to see you, to see the future of our Nation and our Corps. The parade ends when your Senior Drill Instructor gives your platoon the command, "Dismissed!"

You are a United States Marine.

*   *   *

Parting Shots and Saved Rounds

Do not think of graduation as an ending, but a beginning. You are embarking on a new career, a new life. As a recruit, I found the

Pass in Review during Graduation Parade.

more I learned about Marine history, the less I thought about home and the more I thought about my future. It is a strange phenomenon. The logic would seem to flow that the more great deeds I heard about from Marines, the smaller I should feel by comparison. That isn't true in The Corps. Their deeds make us all bigger. The Corps has no "special" units. We are all Marines.

Continue to build your character. That is what wins in combat and what wins in life. Your Drill Instructors set an example for you, but they will not go with you when you leave the Depot. You will have many more leadership examples in the Fleet. Observe your NCOs, officers, and peers. Watch their leadership styles, pick out the best traits, and emulate them. Think of it as putting more tools in your tool bag. Your tool bag will become your leadership style, and it will be unique because it is a combination of tools. You cannot copy this—you must build your own. And never think you have a complete tool bag—be a life-long character builder.

The world is not a perfect place, and neither is the Corps. The difference is, in the Corps you always have an opportunity to change it. As you leave Recruit Training and arrive at subsequent units, beware of the "strap-hangers." These are substandard Marines who do not attempt to raise their performance, but rather attempt to drag you down to their level. Some are clever and will tell you, "That's how it really is out here." They are taking advantage of the fact that you are new. But there is no different set of rules from what you were taught on the Recruit Depot, so don't fall for it. And, as a bonus, you are absolutely authorized to correct them—make them rise to your level instead.

Make sure you leave the Recruit Depot understanding how to solve the moral dilemma. It is impossible for the Corps to teach you all the right answers for all circumstances. Instead, we taught you how to determine the right answer for yourself and to have the courage to do it. So, when confronted with a situation as a Marine, quickly establish what is wrong and eliminate it from your options. Calmly and quickly establish what you are trying to accomplish (your mission). Use initiative and your individual talents to make a decision. Execute that decision without fear of making a mistake.

One last order, Marine: always remember Semper Fidelis, "always faithful"—to God, the country, and The Corps.

Index

About the Author

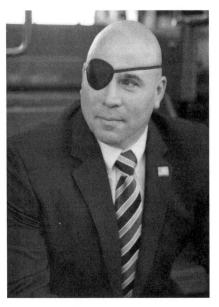

Nick Popaditch ("Gunny Pop") was born on July 2, 1967, in East Chicago, Indiana. After graduating high school, he enlisted in the U.S. Marine Corps at the age of 18, and spent the next three years rotating between South Korea, Okinawa, mainland Japan, and Camp Pendleton, California. During that time, Nick became a tank commander.

Nick's unit was one of the first to deploy in defense of Saudi Arabia. During Operation Desert Shield / Storm, Sgt. Popaditch served at the tip of the spear in Task Force Papa Bear. He commanded an M60A1 main battle tank and participated in the clearing of two minefields and the attack through the heart of the Iraqi defenses. Once back home, he married April and began a family.

After six years of honorable and faithful service, Nick moved into the civilian world, where he worked as a construction worker in Southern California and as a Correctional Officer for the state of Indiana. Nick and April missed life in the Corps, however, and in 1995 Nick reenlisted. After commanding an M1A1 main battle tank, he requested orders to Marine Corps Drill Instructor School, one of the most challenging assignments in the military. He graduated with honors, was promoted to Staff Sergeant, and wore the coveted black belt of a Senior Drill Instructor.

SSgt Popaditch served two combat tours in Operation Iraqi Freedom. He commanded a tank on the march up to Baghdad, was promoted to the rank of Gunnery Sergeant, and served as a tank commander and platoon sergeant in Fallujah. He was awarded the Silver Star for valor during the first Battle of Fallujah, where he was wounded in action. Nick was medically retired in 2005 due to wounds sustained in combat.

"Gunny Pop" speaks to law enforcement agencies, schools, corporations, and churches across the nation on a wide variety of military and motivational issues. He also serves his community as a Mentor/Instructor at the Midwest Marines Focus Program. Nick recently graduated Magna Cum Laude from San Diego State University with a degree in social science.

Nick is the author (with Mike Steere) of *Once a Marine: An Iraq War Tank Commander's Inspirational Memoir of Combat, Courage, and Recovery* (Savas Beatie, 2008), an award-winning title that earned a prominent position on the Commandant's Reading List for the USMC.

Nick and April live in Chula Vista, California, and have two children, Richard and Nicholas.